A Beginner's Guide to the PC Cult

The New War of Religion

by
Sin City Milla

www.sirius.reviews

This book is intended as scholarly analysis, educational research, criticism, opinion, and commentary. Citation of sources relies on Fair Use in 17 U.S. Code § 107, which states that use of copyrighted material "for purposes such as criticism, comment, news reporting, teaching (including multiple copies for classroom use), scholarship, or research, is not an infringement of copyright."

ISBN: 979-8-218-12973-6

CONTENTS

CHAPTERS   **PAGE**

1   INTRODUCTION   1

2   GLOBAL NATURE OF THE CULT   9

3   WHITE GENOCIDE   13

4   THE PARTY LINE   23

5   THE MARKETING MACHINE   39

6   THE ROLE OF ETHNICITY   55

7   HOLLYWOOD   62

8   ACADEMIA   87

9   ORIGINS OF THE CULT   105

10 MAIN FACETS OF THE CULT   116

11 SOCIALISM & COMMUNISM   149

12 WHERE HAVE ALL THE CHRISTIANS GONE?   159

13 JUDAISM & ISLAM   184

14 AFTERTHOUGHTS: THE CORONAVIRUS   196

15 BIBLIOGRAPHY   200

All men by nature desire knowledge.

—Aristotle

This is wrong because there are no, and can never be, true atheists. Humans without religious myth are the ultimate contradiction in terms.

—Sin City Milla

1
INTRODUCTION

What is the PC Cult? P.C. stands for Politically Correct. A cult is any organization based on faith that looks to permanent leaders for answers to every question regarding good and evil. The PC Cult is composed of Social Justice Warriors (SJWs) who look to an established coterie of irremovable leaders for answers to their moral questions.

What does it mean to be a Social Justice Warrior? It means to join the Least Generation. It means to refuse to think, study, or learn as a point of pride, but to accept only pronouncements from their entrenched and irremovable leaders. It means to interpret the world, history, and humanity through a litmus test of inflexible moral values, judging everyone and everything by a morality that admits no error, no opposition, no development, no terminus, dividing the world now and forever into the saved versus the damned. In short, SJWs are members of a religion, sometimes called the Religion of Political Correctness or the Diversity Cult. They are true believers in a global and globalist cult waging a jihad against reason, science, and civilization.

Just as the uninformed and uneducated do not realize that they are uninformed and uneducated (the Dunning-Kruger Effect), SJWs, although they consider themselves 'Woke', or politically conscious, do not realize they are members of a politicized religious cult. But they can be identified by what they say and do.

To be an SJW, one must first have a moralistic bent, classifying not just people as good or evil, but nature itself, subjecting even science and the universe to one's moral judgment. Second, one must claim to be scientific but be highly selective in what one accepts as scientifically proven or as to what constitutes scientific evidence. The moral bent of SJWs serves as a filter, allowing through just enough weakly demonstrated evidence to support their claim to be scientific, while ignoring extensive evidence that is more scientifically valid.

A key part of the SJW mentality is being immunized against facts that are disapproved by the tenets of the PC Cult, defiantly oblivious although conclusively proven by decades of scientific research. Despite what Cultists claim, its tenets are not just unscientific, but anti-science, because to be an SJW is to always put feelings and sympathy before facts. SJWs do not believe in facts. They believe literally that feelings are primary and create facts.

SJWs do not hesitate to lie, cheat, steal, ostracize, ignore legal rights, censor, de-platform, shout down, stuff ballot boxes, assassinate elected figures, reject elections, nullify laws in juries, destroy constitutions, damage statues and public property, loot, and form armed lynch mobs to assault opponents and neutral observers, at times assaulting even other SJWs who may be seen as insufficiently enthusiastic or who have strayed from the PC religion's 'Party Line' by thinking, studying, and learning. For example, in 2017 the SJW Professor Bret Weinstein was forced out of Evergreen College by more militant SJWs who later hunted uncooperative students on the campus at night using baseball bats.

The armed Antifa mobs that infest the streets of many American cities are the Cult's well-funded street militia, organized by Cult college professors and dressed in what has come to be the standard SJW black uniform deliberately reminiscent of Italian Fascist uniforms and the German Nazi SS. SJWs support the growing nation-wide epidemic of black on white crime by dignifying it under the slogan 'Black Lives Matter', deliberately implying that white lives do not, and proving this by tearing up signs that say 'White Lives Matter', 'Blue Lives Matter', or 'All Lives Matter'. Plainly, with SJWs, all lives don't matter – only theirs.

In 2016, an SJW attempted to assassinate a dozen Republican Congressmen at a baseball game, seriously injuring Congressman Steve Scalise before the SJW hitman was killed by police. The attack on the country music festival in Las Vegas in 2017, which killed 58 and wounded several hundred concertgoers, was a planned attack by one or more SJWs. The name Sin City Milla is intended as a reminder of this atrocious attack and its blocked investigation. SJWs hate country music as much as they hate Republican Congressmen as symbolic of traditional American values, and SJWs assume that anyone who attends a country music festival must be an evil racist and therefore deserves death. Yet another SJW, during a Black Lives Matter protest in Dallas in 2016, assassinated five white police officers and injured nine more with a high-powered sniper's rifle in yet another "mostly peaceful protest".

Violence is endemic to the PC Cult and to SJW behavior, the strange death of Supreme Court Justice Antonin Scalia possibly their work as a clandestine attempt to achieve a majority of SJWs on the Supreme Court, not to mention the suspicious deaths of at least a half dozen right-of-center political figures and whistle-blowers in recent years: Andrew Breitbart, Michael Hastings, Bre Payton, Isaac Kappy, Seth Rich, and Rep. Jim Jordan's young nephew Eric Stikley, who died while driving alone on a deserted road when Republican Congressman Jim Jordan was publicly investigating FBI corruption in Congress. Stikley's death was perhaps intended as a warning from the Cult-infiltrated FBI to Jim Jordan to back off his congressional investigation.

Unlikely heart attacks, absurdly unlikely 'suicides', mysterious illnesses, and crashes on lonely roads while driving alone are common scenarios in the deaths of up-and-coming conservative figures not yet famous enough to make front page news. And not only recent – Lee Harvey Oswald was an early SJW, and even earlier versions of today's SJWs may have been responsible for the mysterious deaths of General Patton in 1945 and Senator Joseph McCarthy in 1957. The 'suicide' of conservative writer Francis P. Yockey in 1960 while in jail is also suspicious. The stabbing of Brazil's presidential candidate Bolsonaro by a Brazil-ian SJW while campaigning was more than a warning – Bolsonaro spent weeks in hospital, but like Scalise, survived and went on to win Brazil's presidential election by a landslide.

The Cult has a favorite phrase reflecting its Party Line: 'Diversity is our strength'. Since this phrase has no basis in fact, ethnic diversity in fact weakening states and societies as demonstrated by millennia of historical experience, the phrase is actually a religious catechism, an article of unquestioned and unquestionable blind faith. Agreement with the phrase 'Diversity is our strength' is the first sign that one is dealing with an SJW and a member of the PC Cult. The second sign is reacting emotionally and violently when confronted with inconvenient facts. Peaceful compromise and respect for the opinions of others are not part of the mental repertoire of inflexible SJWs. The third sign is pathological altruism – caring so deeply for 'victims' that the SJW insists on sacrificing not only the SJW but family, posterity, and all of society on the altar of the SJW's unbounded sympathy for the alleged 'victim'.

The fourth sign is smearing opponents as 'Nazis' or 'fascists' instead of calling them 'religious heretics', which is the more accurate term. SJWs like to dredge up the terms 'Nazi' and 'fascist' from history because their emotional content distracts from what is actually happening: an attempt by her to excommunicate and socially isolate the target in order to render him defenseless and easier to eliminate so that the SJW will 'feel safe'. 'Him' because the targets of SJW attacks are usually males, and 'her' because a majority of SJWs are female, though far from all. 'Distract' because the terms 'Nazi' and 'fascist' more accurately describe SJWs and the behavior of their PC Cult in their Fascist-style uniforms than the behavior of their targeted victims, the use of these emotional terms being calculated psychological projection by insincere SJWs.

How can the Cult excommunicate someone from an allegedly secular society? It's easy if you're the law. Contrary to the First Amendment, which prohibits the establishment of a state religion in the U.S., the SJW's PC or Diversity Cult is the *official state religion of the United States,* invoked at every official ceremony and taught in every school, having mostly replaced academic instruction about the Constitution or rules-based democratic procedures like Robert's Rules of Order, which are now routinely rejected by SJWs as 'racist', the ultimate PC 'sin'.

From an entrenched position in the federal court system, as promulgated by the Supreme Court and enforced by successive attorneys general and SJW federal attorneys in the Department of Justice, the Diversity Cult has since the mid-1960s been strictly enforced at all levels of government and in every government-accredited college and public school grade. Though the term 'Diversity' was not yet popular in the 1950s, it was already the moral justification for President Eisenhower when he used federalized armed National Guardsmen to enforce racial desegregation in Little Rock, Arkansas. He later said that this was the greatest mistake of his presidency.

The U.S. today is a theocracy ruled by elite members of the PC Cult. With the judicial and executive branches backing Diversity with every means at their disposal, and even the intelligence services infiltrated by Diversity-promoting SJWs (McCabe, Brennan, Comey, Rosenstein, Strzok, Page, Wray, *et al*), and with the legislative branch increasing the applicability and intrusiveness of Diversity and PC legislation in attempts to politicize the most private aspects of daily life, and with the Mass Media and academia amplifying the spread of SJW moral values, SJWs – often showing up as government-subsidized Diversity Enforcement Officers – have become agents of a modern religious inquisition searching out and punishing heretics and dissenters throughout America.

Most heretics, as it turns out, are white males, resulting in a growing purge by Diversity Officers of white males from positions of influence and power throughout the Anglosphere: Europe, North America, Australia, New Zealand, and the few pockets of whites that are permitted to remain in Africa after almost four hundred years of white habitation, which, if whites were treated equally, would make them an indigenous African tribe entitled to international assistance and protection. But SJWs do not treat people equally. Whites, and especially white males, are the only social category from whom SJWs completely withhold their otherwise infinitely indulged, teary-eyed, heart-felt but pathological sympathy.

Removal of influential white males is often done by means of the 'Me-Too' accusation by SJW women. Making a unique exception to state rules of evidence, SJW judges in state courts now regard as admissible the accusations of women entirely unconnected to the plaintiff in a specific case and allow plaintiffs to submit in court suppressed fantasies from their high-school days supported by zero independent evidence – because feelings and sympathy are always more important to SJWs than facts, including to SJW judges. Thus, any public accusation of unwanted touching by a woman – or even implying unwanted touching, a matter of pure subjectivity at the whim of the 'victim' and her perhaps invented memories – can successfully 'Me-Too' a white male out of his job and out of power.

Although sometimes male SJWs, like the movie mogul Harvey Weinstein, are also accused, that is merely collateral damage by a highly useful political tool, which is almost always used only against men with white skin. SJW males often survive a 'Me-Too' accusation – Disney's Pixar executive John Lasseter, for example, is back on the job despite multiple harassment allegations. Non-SJW males, however, once accused, are *never* allowed to return to their job or career, for example, Nobel prize winners James Watson and Tim Hunt.

The purpose of SJWs' 'Me-Too' tactic and their often invented incidents is to remove white males from power. Or, if they have no power, to silence them and make of them an example to intimidate other white males, as with the false rape charges brought against Julian Assange, against high school football players, or even against poor whites who have no influence to lose.

2
GLOBAL NATURE OF THE CULT

Though the term SJW is American in origin, the Cult is not limited to the United States. The Cult is explicitly global in scope. Cult members have no loyalty to any particular nation or state, but only to their international, indeed anti-national, global and globalist PC movement. Similar Inquisitions have taken hold in Australia and in Europe, where the Cult has been adopted by several European nations and by the European Union as their own state religion.

The international nature of the Cult serves to coordinate these Inquisitions across national boundaries, as when Cult members in Britain's MI6 intelligence service delivered fake documents to their eager Cult brethren in the FBI (Strzok and Page) in a coordinated bid to execute an illegal *coup d'etat* against the heretic Trump, who seemed at the time about to challenge the entrenched state privileges of the Cult. The Cult members' loyalty to each other in their coup attempt proved stronger than their loyalty to Britain or to the U.S.

Cult members have no loyalty whatsoever to the nations of their birth and feel no obligation to abide by the results of any merely *national* election – their loyalty is always *exclusively* to the global PC Cult, dual citizenship popular among Cult members as a point of pride, and treason to the nation-state of their birth seen as a moral duty.

Cult members have also penetrated the United Nations and international institutions as the Cult's tenets become embedded in International Law, primarily under the sponsorship of Professors of Human Rights law who teach in American Ivy League universities, the Ivy League Ground Zero for the Cult as a mass movement, with university Ethnic & Gender Studies departments and campus 'safe spaces' serving as the PC Cult's 'mosques' in the launching of their global PC Jihad.

Human Rights law is the primary vehicle by which Cult moral values acquire the force of law internationally, the list of such 'human rights' continually expanding as Cult influence grows. New 'human rights', for example entirely arbitrary changes in language and grammar, are invented regularly out of thin air by the Ivy League priests of the PC Cult and added to their ever-growing list of so-called 'rights' without ever consulting the public, but only other SJW professors who are personally dedicated to expanding the PC agenda.

As a result, the scope of the Diversity Cult has gone far beyond race and gender, and if not resisted, will eventually include female circumcision, plural marriage in many permutations, post-birth 'abortion' with organ marketing, incest, pedophilia, infant penile excision, and transgender abortion rights (sic). You can set your clock on when these will be 'discovered' in the U.S. Constitution by the SJW members on the Supreme Court with elaborate explanations by wealthy SJW-controlled private foundations like the MacArthur and Ford and Gates Foundations on how the Founders really did put these 'rights' in the U.S. Constitution, although unsuspected by previous Supreme Courts for two and a half centuries and still invisible to everyone but the 'woke' SJW judges who serve in the federal judiciary.

While the West has largely succumbed to the Cult, with its most powerful institutions infiltrated and compromised, a few countries have so far resisted: post-Communist Russia under Putin, Hungary under President Orbán, Estonia, Latvia, Lithuania, Iran, South Korea, China, and Japan. Several of these countries have therefore become the target of a virulent Mass Media hate campaign from Cult-dominated Western media and Cult-dominated globalist institutions, sometimes accompanied by extreme economic sanctions designed to force 'regime change' in those countries by starving their people in a slow-motion death-by-blockade. Since the start of the Ukraine war, Russia and Iran in particular have been prime targets of this illegal treatment, with stern warnings to China and Hungary to stay neutral, while the Baltic countries along with Ukraine under Zelensky are now inviting Cult values into their countries as a requirement of accepting Nato defense.

Extreme economic sanctions have long been considered an act of war that was beneath the dignity of civilized nations since these are directed not against governments but against the health and welfare of civilian populations, but now genocidal sanctions are pursued routinely as normal peacetime policy by Cult-dominated Washington DC. The results have been not only to inflict enormous harm on the people of the targeted countries, and to propel the world repeatedly into crises that threaten a new world war, but to create ever larger numbers of war resisters and anti-war dissidents, edging the new theocratic U.S. and Europe closer to internal chaos as they see their domestic sovereignty and economies eroded by globalist Cult-dominated organizations and global corporations increasingly penetrated by fundamentalist SJWs.

3
WHITE GENOCIDE

The key test for whether a government is controlled by the Cult is whether it permits large-scale immigration from regions closer to the equator, meaning typically a southern border for those countries situated in the northern hemisphere. The word 'Diversity' implies that national borders should be abolished to allow for these southern migrants – who are always termed 'refugees' rather than migrants, again for the distraction afforded by the emotional content of the term 'refugee'.

The Cult's intimate involvement in assisting mass southerly immigration through generous funding of NGOs, and only those NGOs which subscribe to the Cult's Party Line – often by the wealthy SJW George Soros – clearly shows the Cult's anti-national and anti-patriotic agenda. (Soros: "I give away something up to $500 million a year throughout the world promoting Open Society.")

This massive immigration endangers the survival of domestic ethnicities. The word 'Diversity' was chosen by SJWs because it seems to suggest harmonious coexistence of different elements, like a rainbow. But Diversity is not a rainbow. Despite its apparent embracing of differences, it does not preserve differences; on the contrary, the political agenda of the Cult is one world, one government, and one human race in a global digital worker-ant hive, where the individual has no rights but can be freely sacrificed by the moral and economic demands of the PC elites.

In regard to race, Cultists believe that in their future One World Society all ethnicities will merge into a single undifferentiated biological humanity, where each individual will become indistinguishable from every other individual, everyone's skin color – the only biological difference that SJWs ever acknowledge – becoming exactly the same.

This racial merging, however, is not happening today and will not happen in the future. In practice, the natural tendency of all racial and ethnic groups of humans, like all other species, is to perpetuate their own genetics. This means that massive immigration by a different ethnicity ends up not merging with but *displacing* the native ethnic group, resulting in the latter's disappearance, with only a very few 'merging' into the global Hive by marrying outside their own genetic pool.

For most ethnic groups the globalism of the PC Cult means therefore not a peaceful merging but annihilation, and not just of domestic cultures and traditions but *of the people themselves* as they are displaced by foreigners who look, act, and think differently and who are often fully aware that extinction of the domestic group is the unspoken but true agenda of the Cult, interracial marriage usually just as unpopular among most Cult members and immigrants as it is to the targeted group.

SJWs know this and will sometimes admit it. While SJWs insist that there are no distinct human races and that all human biological groups are exactly the same except for superficial skin color, when SJWs are challenged, or when they believe that they have achieved political control, they drop the pretense and admit that whites are in fact being replaced and becoming a minority in the U.S. and Europe and that, in the words of the SJW Joe Biden, *this is a good thing*.

In other words, the Cult uses the One World / One Human Race fantasy as a tool to persuade the targeted domestic ethnicity – which always turns out to be people of European ancestry, or 'whites' – not to resist but to lie down and passively collaborate in their own destruction.

The U.N defines genocide as *the deliberate inflicting of conditions of life calculated to bring about the physical destruction of a race or group in whole or in part*, so 'white genocide' is the correct term to use. Even though most SJWs themselves are white, this genocide of whites world-wide is a prime goal of SJWs in their global Jihad.

The free exercise of abortion, known as abortion on demand as a convenient method of post-coitus birth control, is another prime element of the PC Cult's moralistic agenda of reducing the number of whites since their 'carbon footprint' allegedly harms the Environment and 'rapes the Earth', as if a planet could give or revoke permission for any human activity.

Along with immigration, abortion is another tool the PC Cult uses to annihilate whites, promoting its free use up to, and after, actual birth. In prior, more civilized times, this was called murder. Migrant mothers with babies are far more dangerous to a society than invading soldiers because they give forth progeny; thus, abortion is a far more effective weapon than guns because it renders all future generations extinct. SJWs know this, too.

In the 1970s the globalized corporate Mass Media succeeded

in persuading white women that making money is more rewarding than having children. Abortion in the U.S. has since then been disproportionately used by white women with high IQs as a method of enabling them to pursue careers, lowering the average intelligence of the white population at a much faster rate than non-white populations (described in detail below), even if non-whites may also widely use abortion.

Tens of millions of abortions have occurred in the U.S. since 1973 when early SJWs on the Supreme Court unilaterally and unconstitutionally dictated to the states in *Roe v. Wade* that abortion is a 'Fundamental Right' and that no state may prohibit it, reversing centuries of American law and tradition and ignoring the plain text of the U.S. Constitution. The 5-4 *Dobbs v. Jackson* decision of 2022 by the U.S. Supreme Court which reversed the 1973 *Roe v. Wade* decision will in no way halt SJWs in their efforts not merely to allow abortion on demand throughout the Anglosphere, but to enforce it as a means of genociding whites. Abortion is the ultimate weapon of war and the most effective opening move in any path to conquest – or to social suicide.

Part of the so-called 'right to privacy', which exists nowhere in the Constitution, being another unilateral and unconstitutional *diktat* by unelected Cult members on the Court, abortion has become the prime tool by which globalist corporations ensure a doubling of potential employees at less than half the pay formerly paid to a single male worker and was sufficient to support a wife and several children.

Free abortion on demand paid for by tax-subsidized Planned Parenthood is one of the two primary tools that the Cult uses to impoverish white countries – the other tool is unlimited southerly immigration, which replaces the already declining white population under the destructive impact of abortion while it deliberately reduces wages to subsistence level, the level of hugely over-populated Third World countries.

The media has many techniques for disguising these developments. SJWs habitually refer to whites as 'the Majority' and non-whites as 'Minorities'. These labels – like so much of the linguistic fakery invented by SJWs – are misleading and wrong. In the year 1900, Egypt had a population of 6 million people; Pakistan had 10 million people; Bangladesh perhaps 10 million; Africa as a whole no more than 100 million; India (without Pakistan and Bangladesh) had 300 million; China 400 million. Today, less than 120 years later, Egypt has a population of *106 million and is adding another two million people every year*, Pakistan *has 216 million and is adding two million per year*; and Bangladesh has *165 million and still counting*. It is yet to be seen whether the Ukraine War's interdiction of grain exports will have any impact on this massive global population growth, which has as of now reached 8 billion.

A few locusts are no danger but a swarm of billions is one of the most destructive forces in nature, consuming every resource that people need to survive. A locust swarm of people is what is coming to Europe and the U.S., unleashed by the no-borders Cult. Africa is groaning under the environmental and wildlife destruction caused by *1.5 billion* people, while India and China have grown to 1.3 billion each, causing wholesale irreparable destruction of the environments of those countries.

SJWs trumpet that the rate of growth has slowed – *but it is too late*. The world's oceans are littered with the plastic and human waste dumped by rivers flowing out of these overpopulated and at times ungovernable places, and the world's atmosphere is polluted by the waste and CO2 dumped by their poorly regulated, coal-fired industries, in multiple quantities of what the U.S. has ever produced, and hundreds of millions of people are eager to leave these areas and migrate to white countries legally or illegally.

If that is not enough to be cautious about abolishing borders: Egypt, Pakistan, and Bangladesh – as Muslim countries – remain largely obedient to the injunction of Islamic religious leaders prohibiting all forms of birth control and therefore continue to grow at a high rate, contradicting the popular notion, akin to wishful thinking, that growth rates always slow under urbanization. Sometimes they don't.

India and China have barely paused under the impact of epidemics like the Wuhan Coronavirus and the poverty caused by their overpopulation; and Africa is predicted by population experts to *double* to 3 billion people in the next forty years, despite HIV, Ebola, and the Wuhan Virus. Nigeria alone is expected to reach 500 million, more than the entire United States.

Countries around the world already experience massive illegal immigration from these baby-factories, often discovering shipping containers jammed with sick illegals smuggled in with no inspection for contagious disease or escorted from Africa and Asia by well-funded international criminal organizations directly into 'Sanctuary' cities in the U.S., protected and funded by SJWs like

Joe Biden and George Soros even before arriving at the U.S. border.

These criminal cartels operate like global corporations, complete with swanky offices and billboard ads, to recruit more clients to smuggle into the U.S. or Europe. Libya, in fact, has joined Muslim Mauritania to become a renewed Muslim slave market for Africans who had hoped to be smuggled into Italy, returning Libya to its slave markets of previous centuries – with never a protest from otherwise perpetually morally outraged SJWs, whose only interest is to get them into white countries by any way feasible in furtherance of their agenda of white genocide.

The destination of choice of these migrants – who are 'refugees' only in the sense that they are fleeing masses of other 'refugees' – is *always* temperate-zone countries built and populated by whites. These so-called refugees never 'flee' closer to the equator even when space is available. Saudi Arabia, for example, declines to accept any refugees, but none wish to enter. They always head north to white countries where they can achieve quick citizenship, a status that true refugees searching for safety would care little about.

In 1900, Europe, North America, Russia, and Australia had over 25% of the world's population. Today, these regions have less than 6% of the world's population. While whites are still a majority within most of their own countries, as a percentage of the world's population whites today are less than 4% and shrinking rapidly. Globally – *which is exclusively how SJWs think, and all that matters to them* – whites are a small and shrinking minority subjected everywhere to racial restrictions, legal discrimination, government-promoted drug addiction, and state-subsidized abortion and easy divorce to damage their populations as much as possible in order to reduce their resistance to forcible displacement by equatorial migrants who are not held to the same sets of rules.

The world's non-white population is growing and migrating *at the expense of whites*. Abortion and immigration are the tools; White Genocide is the goal. The PC Cult is responsible and their leaders – including every Democratic and Republican Party presidential candidate for the past fifty years – openly celebrate this result and proclaim their intent to expand it. Indeed, the religious ideology of the anti-white Diversity Cult *demands* it.

1948 Convention on the Prevention and Punishment of the Crime of Genocide (the Genocide Convention): **Article II**: In the present Convention, genocide means any of the following acts committed with intent to destroy, in whole or in part, a national, ethnical, racial or religious group, as such:

    a.   Killing members of the group;

    b.   Causing serious bodily or mental harm to members of the group;

    c.   Deliberately inflicting on the group conditions of life calculated to bring about its physical destruction in whole or in part;

    d.   Imposing measures intended to prevent births within the group;

    e.   Forcibly transferring children of the group to another group.

Each of these acts is currently being committed by the PC Cult against whites throughout the Anglosphere:

(a) In South Africa, SJWs are collaborating in the systematic murder of whites, while in the U.S., whites are subjected to an epidemic of black criminal violence with the full knowledge of police forces and courts which decline to intervene, while the media routinely cover these up and disguise the race of black offenders, calling them 'teens'.

(b) Throughout the Anglosphere, white families are systematically subjected to divorce, and white children, once deprived of a stable home life, are then subjected to mental harm in schools where they are taught that they have no culture, no valid history, and have nothing to be proud of, while their true history – the story of the greatest civilization the world has ever known, Western Civilization, which defined the very concept of human rights – is ignored, vilified, or suppressed.

(c) Throughout the Anglosphere, the theocracies that rule these countries inflict conditions of life, such as Affirmative Action discrimination against whites, which, together with unrestrained immigration, are calculated to bring about their physical destruction.

(d) Throughout the Anglosphere, birth control and abortion are subsidized by the state and heavily promoted in the Mass Media and in state-owned media in an effort to persuade women – and especially intelligent white women – to stop having babies, which constitutes a state-subsidized genocidal policy.

(e) Finally, throughout the Anglosphere, white children are routinely transferred from the custody and control of white families to SJW-controlled 'educational' institutions, where they are indoctrinated in such a way that loyalty to non-whites is substituted for loyalty to whites, with the result that drug addiction and suicide concentrated among white youth become not just predictable but unavoidable.

All of these policies are intentionally promoted by SJW members of the PC Cult with limitless aid from the state.

4

THE PARTY LINE

Why don't whites resist? This strange passivity on the part of whites – especially the white working class and so-called liberals – in their own destruction is accomplished through the PC Cult's exclusive claim to morality. The PC Cult's Party Line is an unofficial but widely promulgated litmus test of undebatable moral values that SJWs and their 24/7 media constantly push.

These moral values are seen by SJWs as universally applicable today, in the past, and forever. In the eyes of SJWs, the Party Line is perfect; when a Cult member dares to think for himself and thus, predictably, gets branded by other SJWs as a heretic, he is required first to publicly admit his error because the Cult can never be seen publicly to be wrong.

The heretic is afterwards, nevertheless, 'excommunicated' – publicly shamed and expelled from the PC movement, and if possible, fired from his job. Examples are the SJW journalist Chris Matthews, who after decades on radio and TV allegedly told a colleague in private "Why haven't I fallen in love with you yet?", which committed the PC sin of sexism by making the SJW woman feel, in her own word, "uncomfortable" (this from a supposed adult woman). And the radio personality Don Imus, who after decades on radio, in a moment of excitement while reporting a basketball game, uttered the words "nappy-headed ho", which committed the PC sin of racism, and he was forced to retire. Both publicly apologized but were fired anyway. . . because that's how SJWs roll.

What are these moral values which SJWs consider so sacred that they cannot be debated, may never be subjected to scientific inquiry, and that – despite their genocidal effect on whites everywhere – cannot be openly discussed without SJWs demanding that the offending 'Nazi' be silenced, ostracized, and legally prosecuted? What are these moral values that neutralize all natural resistance to the deliberate genocide of SJWs' own genetic kin in the face of massive southerly immigration and government-subsidized abortion, along with the destruction of the U.S. government, America's republican institutions, its democratic traditions, its cities, and the physical degradation of the country's environment under the pressure of ever larger numbers of colonizing, often hostile, migrants?

And not only the U.S., but also the Cult-controlled governments of Europe, Australia, Canada, South Africa, and New Zealand, all of which have adopted the same interconnected and mutually assisting Diversity Cult as their official religion, like local branches of a militarized Salvation Army, each president acting like a local satrap executing orders from a central command.

First is 'Equality'. All 'persons' everywhere, now, in the past, and in the future, on planet Earth or on yet to be discovered planets, are regarded as 'equal' in the eyes of Cultists. It doesn't stop there. The term 'persons' includes not only all humans, apes (sic), and aliens (think of the 'the Federation' in the Cultish TV show *Star Trek*), but in the mental universe of SJWs is extended to include even animal and plant life, the definition of 'person' extending to encompass 'Mother Earth', or Nature Herself. Nature is always female in the minds of SJWs, who strangely do not object to gender in this one category.

Thus, as with the word 'Diversity' – which actually means its exact opposite: uniformity – the way SJWs use the word 'Equality' is deceptive. Despite their constant calls for Equality between races or sexes, they do not mean that all persons have equal rights in the Enlightenment sense of every human possessing 'human rights', since obviously Old Growth trees, Darter fish, infectious bacteria, and cattle bred over millennia for human consumption and can no longer survive in the wild, cannot possess human rights. Far from practicing true equal rights, SJWs promote tribalism and exclusive ethnic privilege when they believe it is to their advantage. Only when it comes to policies that might benefit whites do SJWs flip and proclaim: 'But we are all the same!'

On the contrary, any normal definition of the term 'Equality' would be wrong. Even among humans, SJWs insist on the implementation of what is called 'Affirmative Action' for particular groups, which in the U.S. favors by law some groups over others, in employment, government contracts, and acceptance into universities. Sometimes these policies of favoritism are justified by the argument that equality can never be achieved by equal opportunity but only by equal outcome. Democrat President Lyndon Johnson famously demanded equal outcome for blacks when promoting his Great Society program.

Resulting from philosophical assertions by Marx and Nietzsche that there is no Will, free or otherwise, and that therefore none are responsible and none should be held liable for their actions, it is claimed that inequality in income or wealth must be the result of 'institutional racism' or 'systemic sexism' and that only a top-down enforcement of quotas guaranteeing equal outcomes in income, wealth, education, property, and political power can achieve the SJW holy grail of 'Equality'.

Aside from the philosophical issues attached to the doubtful 'No Free Will' claim, the assertion that unequal outcomes must reflect systemic bias rests on the false assumption that all people everywhere are exactly the same, that everyone is born with the same 'blank slate', or *tabula rasa*. Despite the agenda of international corporations, which seek to classify people as interchangeable parts in a global factory-type machine and thus clearly have an interest in promoting this radical egalitarian view, people in fact are demonstrably not the same and therefore not equal in any meaningful sense, and cannot be made equal by any level of government spending, government favoritism, social engineering, or pathological altruism – because in the end, as multiple genetics researchers, psychologists, and biologists have conclusively proven, *genetics ultimately trumps environment*.

Identical twins raised separately in radically different homes do not mature into profoundly different adults but into adults with very similar capabilities, accomplishments, and interests. Chimpanzees raised as humans do *not* act like humans but become neurotic chimps. Men raised as women, even when surgically altered, do *not* become women, but continue to win athletic competitions due to their masculine muscles and will respond physically to perceived threats just as men do – they remain men.

Australian Aborigines and Amerindians, if left to their own de-

vices, on the whole do *not* build peaceful wealthy Western-style
societies, but remain poor, ignorant, and isolated, and are disproportionately prone to alcoholism, obesity, diabetes, child abuse,
and domestic violence. Sub-Saharan Africans, when left to their
own devices, do *not* create a Switzerland or a Singapore, but a
Congo, a Liberia, a Somalia, or a Haiti.

The boundary between Haiti and the Dominican Republic, two
countries with similar histories, can be seen from orbit: the Hait-
ian side is brown and eroded; the Dominican side green and lush.
It is no accident that Haiti, the most biologically African country
in the Western Hemisphere, is the poorest and in every other sense
the most like West African countries, the genetic homeland of virtually all Haitians, unlike Dominica, few of whose inhabitants can
trace their ancestry to Africa.

Whether slavery, racism, or colonialism were in a country's
historical past *turns out to be utterly irrelevant*. South Korea and
Singapore emerged from poverty and colonialism to become
among the best-organized and wealthiest societies in the world in
only two generations, while East and Southeast Asian immigrants
to the U.S. achieved the highest academic honors in only one generation after having fled slavery, war, poverty, military occupation, and colonialism in Asia, thus proving beyond a shadow of a
doubt that the 'institutional racism' which SJWs complain inces-
santly about in the U.S. is a delusion and a fraud and a mere
change of name from 'voodoo'.

But nothing ever penetrates the Cult's inoculation against facts
and science. Far from creating social equality, Affirmative Action,
by permanently promoting certain groups over other groups in all

phases of life, has implemented a *caste system* in the U.S., with white Americans relegated permanently below all non-white domestic ethnicities and below the ever-growing number of non-white immigrants, under laws originated and enforced by congressional members of the globalist and anti-national Cult, and by the SJW judges in the federal courts, who routinely endorse the superior rights of non-whites over whites, of non-Americans over Americans, and – just to make sure whites never unite to defend themselves from the PC Cult's stealth genocide of whites – of white women over white men.

Naive people, not initiated into the gory details of American law and inexperienced in foreign travel beyond trips to the Louvre or London, do not realize how over-populated the non-white world truly is, or that *Affirmative Action also legally applies to foreigners numbering in the billions* who do not speak English, cannot find the U.S. on a map, and who often despise Americans and everything about America.

They too benefit from America's Affirmative Action laws by:

(1) operation of anti-white employment discrimination policies in favor of anyone resident in the U.S., however they got here, including so-called 'asylees' and 'refugees', and unlimited transfers of foreign executives from overseas by multinational corporations (L-1, L-2 visas), which lead directly to U.S. citizenship;

(2) by operation of the Cult-named 'Diversity Visa' overseas lottery system;

(3) by mandatory Minority Business Enterprise policies in municipalities and all levels of government, which require preferential contracting with non-whites, including green-card immigrants

who have not yet – and may decide never to – become U.S. citizens, even if all they intend is to flip their MBE-awarded contracts for a quick profit to white-owned companies; and

(4) by chain migration, as each new citizen or 'anchor baby', even if born this side of the U.S. border in a mere half-hour of 'birth-tourism', becomes entitled when the child turns eighteen to file family petitions for overseas relatives, who then become entitled to file petitions for their relatives, ad infinitum.

This writer has personally been offered city contracts worth many millions of dollars by African immigrants with fake degrees, which they openly admitted they purchased online overnight, and then obtained city contracts via municipal MBE programs and wished only to flip these contracts to white-owned companies for a quick, huge profit.

In other words, the hiring by every American employer of Pakistanis, Egyptians, Liberians, Indians, Somalis, Libyans, Nigerians, Chinese, Tierra del Fuegans, and even billionaire Saudis, if they are resident in the U.S. and have permission to work, over and above the hiring of white American citizens is *required by American law.* These migrants, even if quotas have already been met, can still continue to be hired in preference to white male Americans by SJW employers on the grounds that white male Americans, and only white male Americans, do not fall under any 'protected class' – as defined by the anti-white SJW Cult members on the Supreme Court. 'Protected class' is the euphemism that the SJWs on the Supreme Court employ when they unilaterally establish a permanently superior caste in violation of the plain text of the Fourteenth Amendment to the U.S. Constitution and of

American tradition extending almost 200 years before there was a U.S. Constitution.

The false doctrine that all people everywhere are exactly the same in everything but superficial skin color – that race and gender are invented and mere 'social constructs' – is so ingrained in the vacuum mentality of misinformed SJWs, reflecting their supreme ignorance of biology, that if the borders were abolished and floods of immigrants allowed, SJWs believe that the immigrants would magically become law-abiding, tax-paying, responsible citizens of Western countries simply by taking up residence on American soil, or British soil, or Australian soil, or any other predominantly white country, which SJWs see as Magic Dirt.

In reality, immigrants often form criminal rings based on ethnic solidarity: Nigerians often focus on medical billing fraud; Muslim Arabs often focus on fake traffic accidents to defraud car insurance companies; clannish Indians often indulge in insider trading, showing zero regard for minor things like legalities. This writer has encountered each of these in his law practice.

The high cost of car insurance, Medicare, and housing in the U.S. are directly related to the globalist immigration policies of SJWs, helping to transform what once was a low-crime, peaceful, high-trust U.S. society into today's no-trust, high-cost, crime-ridden society, every grocery item now requiring multiple seals to avoid tampering where formerly none were needed, and every phone number and home address becoming a security issue where formerly such data were available to every U.S. citizen and delivered for free to everyone's front door.

This Magic Dirt theory betrays an ignorance of human societies, history, and crime statistics so deep and profound that one can only conclude that the special faith of SJWs is rooted in more than reason and rationality, their filter against facts, science, and crime statistics operating on the mind of an SJW precisely like an immune response after inoculation against a virus. Facts just can't get in – even if heard, they are rejected by the SJW due to the speaker's alleged 'tone' or because the facts make the SJW 'uncomfortable'. SJWs are thus like ants whose brains have been infected by a fungus that compels them to climb plant stems and suicidally expose themselves to be eaten by birds, thus furthering the life cycle of the fungus at the cost of the ant's life. SJWs know this – but they still climb the stem – and deliberately drag the rest of us with them.

Indeed, some ideas, like the equality of all people and the interchangeability of the sexes in all areas of life, are so self-evidently stupid, even without the mountains of scientific evidence against it, that only intellectuals could believe them. Though perhaps the intellectuals inhabiting the ivory towers of Ground Zero Ivy League universities, the priests of the PC Cult, have other agendas at work than the simple-minded Children's Crusade of One Kumbaya World with One Stereotyped Human Race and One Stereotyped Gender in a One-World Hive – as if even babies not yet capable of speech cannot immediately distinguish a Papuan from a Norwegian, or a woman from a man – which they can.

Equality also directly contradicts Diversity. If everyone is already exactly the same except for skin color, how can there be any true differences to harmonize? The constant, almost desperate, calls of SJWs for Diversity are in fact a reluctant acknowledgment by frustrated SJWs that deep differences do exist, that they are real, and that they are explosive, which explains the panic that ensues when pranksters post innocuous 'It's ok to be white' stickers on school walls, triggering mass demonstrations and hysterical calls for FBI investigations and intervention by armed National Guardsmen. Or when panicked teachers call police and demand an arrest because a six-year-old in kindergarten pointed a finger in imitation of a gun or 'harassed' another six-year-old with a hug.

If true equality is the goal, meaning the merging of all ethnic groups into one so that every individual is interchangeable with every other and thus fit for global factory-style employment, then Diversity would have to be sacrificed. But what we see in practice is the sacrifice *of both Equality and Diversity in the dogma of Intersectionality*: quotas that enforce a ladder of privileges of some groups over others, creating a layered system that incorporate superior immigrant equatorial castes holding the whip hand over inferior native whites as Enoch Powell foresaw.

Under Intersectionality, white males have become a caste of Untouchables in a multi-layered hierarchy supervised and enforced by unelected Cult judges throughout the imperial federal judiciary, who rely on decisions rendered by other unelected Cult members entrenched for life on the Supreme Court – decisions enforced by naive Presidents duped by the Cult's deceptive propaganda of Equality – decisions that were never imagined in their wildest dreams by the congressmen who passed the so-called 'Civil Rights' laws which these Judges Gone Wild brazenly cite when they implement their *personal and unconstitutional* Cultic agenda. The Cult's unacknowledged prophet, Nietzsche, foresaw this: "[There is an] eventual rank-ordering of the diverse elements of the population in every great racial synthesis." [*On the Geneaology of Morality*, 2nd Essay, Sec. 20]

Equality and Diversity conflict because they are different points on a continuum of multiethnic political confrontation. For a particular ethnic group that may long ago have been disadvantaged, the slogan of 'Equality' naturally shifts from (1) independence of that group ('the right to contract'), to (2) achieving a significant level of influence in the political contest ('equal opportunity'), and finally (3) to establishing a system of entrenched privilege ('equal outcome'). However, the formerly disadvantaged group will continue to use the same outdated slogan of Equality from start to finish because it works. It works because their political opponents remain mesmerized by previous, though long obsolete, meanings of the term Equality, still dreaming of Emancipation Proclamations and Underground Railroads as if those remain even remotely relevant today.

The term Diversity appears during the 'equal opportunity' stage (2). For a particular ethnic group that may once have lived under segregation or slavery, and all groups have at some point in their history including whites, the slogan 'Diversity is our Strength' serves to support the shift from Segregation to Desegregation, bringing up pleasant memories of Selma civil rights marches and college Free Speech sit-ins.

Once ethnic groups are thoroughly mixed, however, and legal disabilities removed, the next stage kicks in as Affirmative Action laws are no longer seen as a strictly temporary measure to create a more level playing field, as Congress stated was its intent when first passing those laws in the 1960s, but are reinterpreted as *permanent*, requiring quotas or near-quotas, meaning favoritism and consciously pro-bias. The term Diversity in stage (3) is then reinterpreted to mean equal outcomes, or entrenched privilege – which was not contemplated by Congress when it passed these laws and was scornfully dismissed at the time by the Cultic bills' sponsors as something that could *never, ever happen*.

There is also a Stage (4) to Diversity: the removal of members of the targeted group to make room for the more privileged group as Diversity is increasingly recognized to mean Exclusion in conformity with the true principle of Uniformity pursued by the Cult. This is justified by various artificial historical arguments with selectively chosen 'facts' taught in public schools where the curricula, focused on the false presumptions of a universal blank slate and no free will, are under full Cultic control as the unofficial but very real State Religion.

At this Removal stage, often ironically called 'Inclusion', 'Diversity is our Strength' is taken to its logical limit and becomes 'No Whites Allowed'. Thus, under the SJW agenda, Diversity only becomes complete when the 'No Whites Allowed' sign goes up – the entity is then declared 'fully diverse'. Many businesses, banks, and government offices are already 'fully diverse' in parts of the U.S., not a single white face visible anywhere on the premises. Job applications from whites are rarely accepted by 'fully diverse' enterprises.

If the reader resides in what is still a mostly white geographic area, then this movie is coming soon to a theater near you, and once it arrives will run for the rest of your life. Watching the immigrant wave that is engulfing border states and displacing whites with the encouragement of Washington DC, one can only watch in awe at the naiveté and ignorance of the mostly white Northeast and Mid-West and Pacific coast, who still don't comprehend what will happen to them when waves of disproportionately low-skilled, low-IQ, non-tax-paying, fake-documented immigrants collecting welfare and pocketing stolen IDs crashes over them and they too find themselves forced into unemployment in droves, legally dispossessed by the Supreme Court from every institution – including local schools and government – that their ancestors conceived, designed, paid for, and built *for them*.

The formerly segregated group continues to use the same slogan of Diversity from start to finish because it works. It works because, as with the earlier term 'Equality' (sometimes updated to 'Equity'), their political opponents remain mesmerized and rendered passive by previous, though long obsolete, meanings of the term 'Diversity', with FBI arrests of white-hooded Klansmen and Bob Dylan and Pete Seeger protest songs still dancing in their heads, as if these too remain relevant to today's Cultic Inquisition almost two generations later.

Cult members know that when they use the terms Equality, Equity, and Diversity, they are calling for *not* the preservation or co-existence of the targeted group in a rainbow-like society, whites being the only group that is ever targeted in the U.S., Europe, South Africa, Canada, and Australia – but for whites' eventual *removal*.

Removal of whites to where? There are no countries anywhere, excepting only Russia and a few East European nations, where whites are not already subject to extensive legal disabilities and official racial discrimination – if whites are allowed to immigrate at all, even as genuine refugees. And it is these very countries that are under the pressure of constant war-provoking boycotts and sanctions from Cult-dominated regimes, spearheaded by the U.S., and backed by the European Union, in an effort to force open the borders of these 'heretic' countries to southerly immigration, along with forcing adoption of the other toxic policies calculated to undermine resistance to the Cult, like abortion and gay marriage. If Russia were to allow these Cult policies to operate unopposed throughout the former Soviet Union, the U.S. and EU would halt their military assistance to Ukraine overnight as their ultimate goal of annihilating the last refuges of whites will have been achieved.

One World Power remains the Cult's primary goal, enforcing a racial caste system where the few surviving whites are on the bottom, SJWs remaining totally unconcerned with the individual fates of those who fall victim to their crime-ridden, open-borders, disease-infested, family-destroying, corrupt Anarcho-Tyranny, which is always the practical result of their Cult's 'secular' Jihad.

The contradictions inherent in the mental world of SJWs seem strangely not to affect their daily functioning. Once translated into rational English, 'Diversity' turns out to mean uniformity. 'Equality' becomes inequality. 'Inclusion' becomes exclusion. 'Woke' means asleep. 'Gay' means not 'happy' but growing old alone and childless. Fat becomes fit. Marriage becomes slavery. Whites having children is 'bad for the Earth'. Color, as in 'People of Color,' means black, while the *true* people of color – indigenous Europeans with their many shades of blond, brunet, red, or russet hair and with multiple shades of eye color, from green and blue to olive and hazel, and a variety of skin shades, being the most colorful people anywhere in the world and in all of human history – are told the fantastic lie that they have *no color at all* compared to equatorial black.

'White privilege' turns out to be equally illusory and really means 'uppity whites who haven't got the message that they are now an Untouchable caste on the bottom of society'. The majority is called 'Minorities'. While the true minority – whites – are called 'the Majority'. 'Decolonization', when translated, turns out to mean *colonization* of Europe, the British Commonwealth, and the U.S., and the displacement of their indigenous true people of color by hostile migrants who are entirely devoid of color.

And when childless SJW politicians who aborted whatever white children they had, like Angela Merkel, or self-obsessed, white-hating, pro-abortion, one-child SJWs like Hillary Clinton, fill their nations with millions of illiterate, hostile, corrupt migrants as if they were lonely Cat Ladies filling their empty homes with hundreds of sick, starving cats that fight and crap until their homes become uninhabitable and they feast on the corpse of the deceased host. . . *this* is called acting as a caring world leader providing a heart-felt safe space for 'refugees' who wish no harm to anyone.

Never mind the exploding crime rate, the massacres, the collapsed institutions, the trashed environment, the spreading corruption, the contagious diseases, the scorn for evaporating law and order, the rampant drug abuse, the suicides among young whites, the vanished social capital and trust, and the national bankruptcy that *always* accompany diverse southerly immigration into SJW-ruled subject provinces.

It seems that, for SJWs, it takes a great effort to see what is right under their nose, and that SJWs really do need a weatherman to know which way the wind blows, despite those Bob Dylan songs.

5

THE MARKETING MACHINE

Any evidence that the SJW versions of Equality and Diversity might actually be bad not just for whites but perhaps for everyone, even bad for so-called 'refugees' and bad for the Environment, would undermine the entire powerful apparatus of entrenched privilege that Cult members enjoy in the Anglosphere and Europe. Therefore, such information must be suppressed at all costs.

Any system that is based on lies must suppress the truth. And the Cult, with its almost complete control of the Mass Media, using the greatest marketing machine the world has ever seen, is the source of all lies, the source of the hoax that white males are privileged when they are actually a caste of Untouchables, and the source of the hoax that blacks are disproportionately victims of crime and racism when blacks actually commit the vast majority of violent crime in the U.S. despite being no more than 13% of the population.

So the PC Cult, with its delusions of One Happy World, One Peaceful Human Race, One genderless worker-ant, One Efficient Global Government bringing peace and prosperity to every form of life no matter how small on this and on any other planet, today engages in the most widespread and systematic program of censorship, disinformation, misinformation, and behavioral conditioning that has ever been implemented anywhere.

The Cult's efforts to eliminate free speech grow more pervasive each year and their online collaborators institute the Cult's policies and recommendations ever more efficiently and with ever more coordination, combining not only outright censorship but calculated disinformation, with a goal of flooding the average American – especially echo chamber Feminists, senile 'Boomer' JFK liberals, and tunnel-visioned white male computer programmers who might wake up one day to what the Cult has planned for all whites, *including them* – with such an avalanche of around-the-clock Mass Media conditioning from so many sources and angles and from so many movies and TV shows and concerts and from so many book publishers and fake academics (which are government-subsidized, Cult-controlled, hugely profitable, tax-free global private businesses masquerading as colleges) that it becomes almost impossible for the average person to comprehend the scale of the lying and deception drilled into naive consumers' heads almost from the moment they can hold a cell phone. This has resulted in Americans becoming the most propagandized, censored, and uninformed people in the world, with perhaps the single exception of China.

Most Americans do not realize that most of their information and entertainment comes from only six (6) media companies which are closely interconnected.

I include some detail here to demonstrate the sheer scale and monopolistic nature of the conditioning, which is so influential that it managed to switch almost overnight the color red, which for decades had been the universal color of Communism, with blue. In the 1990s, the Left-wing media snatched blue for themselves and stuck Republicans with the color red just so the Left could avoid the opprobrium of being associated with the crimes of Red Communism, which came to light after the collapse of the Soviet Union in 1991.

Democrats have monopolized blue ever since, while Republicans were forced to accept red. It was not the Republican Party but the Cult's Marketing Machine which made this choice and which perpetuates it. Like the Party Line, the switching of labels is another tradition that the PC Cult inherited from the Communist Party. When the PC Cult labels exclusion 'Inclusion', this is an update of what the Communist Party used to call dialectics, i.e., deliberately lying to gain political power by deception.

The Six Mass Media Companies:

(1) Viacom owns or controls MTV, Nickelodeon, Nick Jr., CMT, BET, Paramount Pictures, TeenNick, Comedy Central, Spike TV, Centric, AddictingGames.com, Shockwave.com, among many other properties.

(2) Disney owns or controls Disney theme parks, ABC, Daytime, ESPN, Vice, History Channel, Lifetime, SEC Network (college sports), Freeform, Touchstone Pictures, Polaris, Pixar, Miramax, Marvel, Lucasfilm (*Star Wars* franchise), GameStar video game developers, and controlling interests in publishers of comic books and science-fiction novels, water sports parks, and 21st Century Fox, which itself includes National Geographic, FX, Twentieth Century Fox Film, Fox Searchlight Pictures, Blue Sky Studios, and Roku, among many others.

(3) TimeWarner owns or controls CNN, HBO (*Game of Thrones* franchise), TimeLife, Turner Broadcasting, TNT, TBS, Cartoon Network, Cinemax, NBA.com, NCAA.com, TMZ.com,

Adult Swim, Bleacher Report, Fandango, Warner Bros., Looney Tunes, The CW, Hulu, niche programming for medical waiting rooms, DC Comics, comic book movie adaptations like Batman, NetherRealm (*Mortal Kombat*), Rocksteady Batman games, WaterTower Music, Warner Music Group, TimeWarner Cable, Otter Media), among many other properties.

(4) Comcast owns or controls NBC, MSNBC, CNBC, Universal Pictures, Focus Featured, AwesomenessTV, Big Idea Xfinity, MLB Network, Comcast Sports, Telemundo, Sky PLC, Dreamworks, E!, Bravo, Sprout, U.S.A Network, Syfy Channel, Philadelphia Flyers, Golf Channel, Oxygen, Buzzfeed, Tastemade, Vox, TheVerge, SB Nation, Easter, Recode, Polygon, Curbed, The Weather Channel, FanDuel, Instacart, TuneIn, Houzz, Nextdoor, Flipboard, Slack, Zola, among others.

(5) CBS owns or controls Showtime, Smithsonian Channel, NFL.com, *Jeopardy*, 60 Minutes, and many more properties.

(6) NewsCorp owns Fox News, FX, Fox Music, Wireless Group PLC, HarperCollins book publishers (includes Christian-niche Zondervan), Stoxx, Dow Jones, SmartMoney, 120 newspapers in five countries, including the *Wall Street Journal, New York Post, The Sun, The Australian*, among others.

These six media entities are controlled by only around 230 executives in interlocked collaborating directorates, guaranteeing that a uniform diet of Cult-approved programming will be almost unavoidable by most of the public wherever they go, 24/7, cradle to grave.

The reach of the most powerful executives and their agendas is in fact even greater than the above suggests, resulting in even more monopolization and uniformity. For example, Sumner Redstone, CEO of Viacom (recently deceased), personally owns not only almost all of both Viacom and CBS, but also 100% of another giant media entity, National Amusements, which in turn owns 950 movie theaters, Simon & Schuster book publishers, and CBS Interactive, which itself runs multiple gaming websites, video game news, and sports news, and GameSpot, Metacritic, CNET, and 247-Sports.

SJWs love to claim that NewsCorp is 'conservative'. But NewsCorp's Rupert Murdoch, although personally by reputation a conservative, which ordinarily means perhaps not being a member of the Cult, sold his entity 21st Century Fox to Disney for $52 billion in 2018, which could not have happened had 21st Century Fox been incompatible with the PC Cult's globalist agenda.

NewsCorp, as judged from its flagship cable channel Fox News, has been in almost lock-step with the Cult's values of so-called Equality and Diversity since its inception, serving as milquetoast controlled opposition, despite Fox being SJWs' favorite whipping boy, the so-called exception of Fox allegedly proving that the Cult is not 100% in control of the media, when in fact it almost is. All NewsCorp properties champion the Cult dogmas of fake Diversity and pretend Equality.

NewsCorp, for example, never gives airtime to the following topics, which are absolutely prohibited by all Cult-run, Cult-owned, or Cult-influenced media entities:

- race realism;
- white genocide;

- the devastating effect of Affirmative Action on the white working class;
- the negative consequences of Cult activities anywhere in the world that they are implemented;
- the abortion epidemic among intelligent white women, resulting in the lowering of white IQs;
- the devastating impact on fathers of free abortion on demand without the father's consent;
- the impoverishment of families due to Feminism;
- the black on white crime epidemic with its covered-up mass shootings by blacks, of Flash lynch mobs by blacks against Asians and Asian-owned stores, and of the black Knockout Game against elderly whites;
- the ineffectiveness of the de-incarceration and no-bail movements in preventing blacks convicted of violent crimes against whites from returning to inflict more crimes against whites, even while wearing court-assigned ankle bracelets;
- the role of the Jewish Sackler family in creating and profiting from OxyContin;
- the possible role of non-white doctors in pushing Oxy-Contin on poor whites, thereby deliberately or negligently creating the opioid epidemic;
- ethnic cohesion among non-white ethnic groups compared to the lack of ethnic cohesion, enforced by law, among whites;
- the connection between weak national borders and falling working class income;
- the connection between abortion on demand and falling middle-class income;

- the connection between expanded welfare among blacks and the decline of the black family;

- the connection between the increased absence of black fathers and the increase in black crime;

- how to protect youth from the poisonous conditioning of unrestrained Big 6 media programming;

- the dramatic decline of youth morals after the breaking of the Motion Picture Production Code (Hays Code) in the 1960s by Hollywood moguls;

- the role of the Big 6 in the explosion of online pornography accessible to children;

- the suicide epidemic among white teens as a result of non-stop exposure to Big 6 media programming;

- the suicide epidemic among veterans as a result of their degradation, ostracism, and expulsion by SJWs from Cult-run colleges, where veterans are routinely insulted and given undeserved poor grades;

- the connection between free sex and emotional demoralization and suicide among young people;

- protection of young boys from the child abuse of gender confusion and physical mutilation encouraged by Big 6 media and transsexual networks;

- any hint of promoting heterosexuality and protecting the family from global pedophile and predatory homosexual networks.

Not one peep from NewsCorp about any of these issues – nor from any of the other Big 6 media empires which profit from *pro-*

moting the above social ailments – or from any Presidential candidate for the past fifty years of any major party. Indeed, just to find information about these suppressed topics, one must go online and pay expensive subscription fees to access obscure scientific journals, or roam the internet, digging through the many obstacles and layers of misdirection imposed by the Big 6 in their efforts to prevent public discussion of genuine public issues.

In 2018, AT&T, whose DirectTV already has a huge presence in the U.S. and Latin America, bought TimeWarner for $85 billion, giving AT&T control of both content and delivery, adding it to its Cricket Wireless, U-verse, Sky Brasil, and TP.com properties, giving Cult values yet another global venue. Also important to the global dimension of the Cult is the supremely SJW entity Univision, which besides its TV and radio and digital assets, owns Fusion, The Onion, The Root, Jalopnik, Jezebel, Deadspin, Lifehacker, Kotaku, and Uforia, among others.

Sometimes regarded as a 6th or 7th member of the top-ranked media empires, Sony owns Columbia Pictures, TriStar, Destination, Fable, Triumph, and Screen Gems. While Sony is Japanese, unlike the other media empires which are all American-headquartered companies, Sony has no interest in challenging, whether in entertainment or news, what is obviously the official state religion of the U.S., which could be business suicide for a foreign-owned entity, and Sony's media executives in the U.S. are in fact mostly Hollywood-connected executives who are closely connected to the executive boards of the other Big 6.

Then there is Verizon, which owns Verizon Wireless, Fios, AOL, Yahoo, Tumblr, HuffPost, Engadget, TechCrunch, Makers,

Build Studios, Rivals.com, Ryot, go90, and Terremark, all of which are also in lockstep not only with the Cult's anti-white values of Diversity and Equality, but with its caste-ridden political agenda which has made whites into Untouchables.

Next is the Associated Press (Chairman **Steven Swartz**), an unincorporated not-for-profit association of 263 news bureaus consisting of the majority of newspapers and radio stations in 106 countries, headquartered in the Cult's geographic center – New York City. AP articles consist of basic 'facts', with the rest of the 'inverted pyramid' supplied by the local affiliate, providing broad opportunities to inject Cult values and fictional elements into every article or radio broadcast, if the AP's New York headquarters by some miracle fails to include them.

The so-called competition to AP is Thomson Reuters, which provides news and real-time stock market data to global customers with over $13 billion in recent annual revenue. Historically Reuters was owned by the Jewish Rothschild banking family, famously alerting Nathan Mayer Rothschild of the news of Napoleon's defeat at Waterloo in 1815, enabling him to make a killing in the London Stock Exchange. In recent times no single individual was allowed to own more than 15% of Reuters PLC, but in 2008 the Thomson family bought 53%, creating Canada-registered Thomson Reuters. In 2018, the Thomsons, Canada's richest family, sold 55% of Thomson Reuters to New York City-based Blackstone Group LP under CEO **Stephen A. Schwarzman** (not to be confused with **Steven Swartz** of the AP).

Blackstone is the largest single owner of real estate in the world, purchasing huge tracts of rental houses and owning motel chains such as Motel 6. Blackstone is also the largest asset manager in the world with a portfolio in 2019 of $880 billion (Wikipedia) and many trillions by 2021. This Jewish-run private equity firm is closely tied to the Democratic Party. Blackstone Group owns 50% of New York City-based Blackrock, the second largest asset manager in the world. Both engage in what is termed shadow banking as asset management firms lend trillions while avoiding direct supervision of banking regulators since they are not technically banks. There is reason to believe that the Jewish Rothschild banking family, the wealthiest banking family in the world, regained control over Reuters via its resale to Blackstone.

Then there are the online giants: Facebook, Amazon, Apple, Netflix, and Google (FAANG), not to mention Twitter and Pay-Pal. The former are increasingly involved in producing entertainment to their online customer base in addition to their control of fake algorithm-written online 'news'.

To illustrate the interlocked nature of most of these allegedly competing media companies: Disney, 21st Century Fox, Time-Warner, and Comcast all have stakes in Hulu, which is delivered to its TV customers via Amazon's FireStick. Disney and the allegedly 'conservative' 21st Century Fox have stakes in the highly 'Progressive' Cult-favorite Vice Media. Disney has stakes in the ultra-liberal and highly censored A&E, History, and Lifetime cable channels, which are ostensibly owned by rival media empires. CBS has a stake in TimeWarner's The CW. Viacom has a stake in Disney's Roku. Verizon has stakes in Complex Media, RatedRed.com, Awesomeness TV, and Seriously TV.

Amazon, which owns Whole Foods, Echo, FireTV, Kindle,

Audible, Twitch, Freevee (formerly IMDb), Goodreads, Abe-Books, ComiXology, DPReview, and Zappos, also has a stake in Instacart.

And Google, which owns YouTube, Android, Chrome, Nexus, Pixel, Google Home, Blogger, Zagat, Nest, Waze, Verily, Gmail, Maps, Hangouts, and Project Fi, also has stakes in supposedly independent Giphy, Medium TuneIn, Slack, Uber, Lyft, Confide, and in Comcast's NextDoor.

And Facebook owns all or part of WhatsApp, Instagram, Oculus, and Internet.org.

The Internet giants are full partners in the Big 6's censorship efforts. Since mid-2017, Google, YouTube, Amazon, Twitter, Facebook, Apple, Instagram, Godaddy, Reddit, Joyent, Patreon, Mailchimp, Blogspot, Wordpress, Stripe, and PayPal have acted in concert to de-platform conservatives, white nationalists, heretics, and dissidents (these are synonymous terms to the Cult) who ask inconvenient questions, and rendering them into Untouchables, deprived of their supposedly constitutionally guaranteed legal rights. We have yet to see whether Elon Musk's acquiring of Twitter will reduce its participation in global censorship or will simply cause it to implode as Twitter itself comes under organized boycott by the Big 6 and their online collaborators.

Many of these companies have united to *de-platform the same person in a single day*, as near as this writer can tell always a white male, which is a blatantly unconstitutional and anti-competitive practice and a form of Bill of Attainder explicitly prohibited by the U.S. Constitution, given that these giants effectively perform governmental functions like delivering mail.

Since online presence has become the new Commons of modern society, essential to preserving society's rights to free political speech, de-platforming is the modern equivalent of cutting out the tongues of slaves, making the First Amendment obsolete and powerless – as SJWs have done with the rest of the Constitution and its Bill of Rights, which as detailed below, SJWs have absolutely no use for or interest in.

These online giants are also deeply involved in creating their own fiat currency, like 'Facebook dollars', to compete directly with the U.S. dollar – another step in the Cult's goal of a global online Hive where Untouchables will be entirely de-personed, a uniquely modern form of imprisonment since new homes have their domestic services and even their door-locks under internet control, which means ultimately by FAANG.

Despite their faux outrage over alleged Russian interference in American elections, these companies have themselves intervened in the elections of multiple countries by de-platforming entire political parties during elections.

For example, Facebook and Instagram suspended the accounts of the Italian political parties CasaPound and Forza Nuova during a recent election. A judge in Italy ordered Facebook to pay restitution for this illegal intervention in Italian elections, but the damage was done. Facebook and Twitter also suspended the accounts of the Irish political party Saoradh, again interfering illegally in a national election, showing these companies' contempt for democratic due process, which is a violation of long-established international law, while projecting their own illegal activities onto mostly non-existent 'Russian bots'.

As part of this process of de-personing, Chrome, Firefox, and most of the other online browsers have begun fraudulently branding dissident websites as malware or hacker sites, which is the online equivalent of calling someone a Nazi, the intent being to ostracize and deny them funding and employment, very similar to what used to happen when the Communist Party of the former Soviet Union would purge dissident Party members, which had the effect of ostracizing them and revoking their food ration privileges. This condemned them to unemployment and possible starvation since both private employment and the private sale of food were illegal in the early Soviet Union.

With SJWs and the legal and social dominance of their PC Cult among the media giants, the 'Party Line', a term invented a century ago by the global Communist Party to justify expelling dissidents, has come to Main Street America – newly armed with powerful online tools that enable action entirely outside government jurisdictions which are restricted by national borders. The online giants are not restricted by geography but are by their nature global, increasingly behaving like a global government more powerful than any nation, including the U.S., and capable of whipping lesser nations into line like sheep.

Their mindset stuck in the last century, the U.S. federal judiciary, however, has consistently declined to intervene in the Big 6 and Internet giants' end-run around the Constitution and monopolistic control of virtually all information that reaches the American public's eyes and ears – including the information that reaches the eyes and ears of Congressmen, Senators, Supreme

Court Justices, and the President. This de-personing has rendered invisible and silenced previously popular anti-SJW figures, often white males who had enjoyed the support of large numbers of on-line subscribers, even millions, until guillotined by the Cult by being de-platformed overnight in concert.

The Sherman Antitrust Act is a clear casualty of the PC Cult's takeover of global transmission of information. The Supreme Court has shut its eyes to the Antitrust Act's burial, as with the rest of the U.S. Constitution and its Bill of Rights. As a sign of the times, Goldman Sachs, the largest investment bank in the world, headquartered in New York City, recently announced that it would no longer arrange IPOs to take firms public if their Board of Directors consisted only of white males, thus enforcing on its own the Cult's unconstitutional religious dogma of Intersection-ality. Boards of Directors may, however, consist only of Jewish males or black males without thereby violating Goldman Sachs' new rule – see below.

This means that the Cult now possesses so much monopolistic power in the U.S. that they can force people to adopt the Cult's moral values *by boycotting their own customers*. Even this clear monopolistic practice has failed to alert the moribund Supreme Court that competition has vanished at the highest levels in the U.S. and that the Sherman Antitrust Act and the Fourteenth Amendment, along with the First Amendment, are dead letters.

Even Visa / Mastercard with Stripe and other online financial services companies have joined this digital lynching of white males, with traditional banks, such as JP Morgan Chase, Wells Fargo, and BBVA, arbitrarily shutting down victims' bank accounts and temporarily freezing their private funds after they have been de-platformed, with – once again – no investigation of this behavior from federal authorities or an injunction by any federal court, yet without slowing for a moment the string of injunctions issued by federal judges who blocked President Trump from closing the U.S. borders to the massive immigration that is replacing whites. Under President Biden, the tit-for-tat dueling between pro and anti-border federal judges continues apace.

If this does not amount to unconstitutional monopoly and a totalitarian abuse of power by quasi-governmental entities acting illegally as an unofficial branch of the U.S. government in enforcing America's illegal and unconstitutional State Religion – speaking here as an attorney who has argued constitutional law in federal court – then I don't know what is. These global corporations, increasingly taking on the appearance of a single global information entity with control over both domestic and international finance, are doing what only totalitarian despotic governments such as the Soviet Union had formerly tried to implement.

This indirect enforcement of Cultic moral values and its anti-white global racial caste system saves the internally compromised U.S. government from getting its hands dirty, which might otherwise trigger a Constitutional crisis in which the Supreme Court would be forced to examine the Cult's status as a state religion that has reduced the U.S. and the Anglosphere to subject provinces of an incipient global PC Cult government.

Why is the Court so reluctant to acknowledge these developments and restore the First, Fifth, and Fourteenth Amendments or the Sherman Antitrust Act? Because the Supreme Court is too compromised by so-called 'conservative' Justices like Chief Justice Roberts who are actually sympathetic to Cult values and by the presence of a long series of outright treasonous SJW Left-Wing Justices, who systematically blocked every attempt for decades to recover national sovereignty and a secular government, in open violation of their oaths to support the Constitution which they took when they became Justices.

Unfortunately, the Cult members who still sit on the Court, together with pro-Cult sympathies shown by several other Justices like Roberts, show every sign of continuing their sabotage for so long as they are permitted to occupy their seats-for-life in violation of their oaths. Lying to obtain a seat on the Supreme Court, as throughout the federal judiciary, in order to exercise supreme power bypassing all electoral and representative institutions, is SOP for SJWs.

6
THE ROLE OF ETHNICITY

This writer was raised in the far-left Progressive Unitarian Church. Unitarianism, now the even more globalist Unitarian-Universalist Church, is so close to Judaism that the Church is often called the Joo-nitarian Church. From a young age, this writer was surrounded by Marxists and Feminists, including many Jews, and was raised devoid of ethnic prejudice, on the contrary becoming by my twenties a dyed-in-the-wool Marxist, Feminist, black rights supporter, and Believer in the Holocaust and the Eternal Victimhood of Jews, women, and 'people of color' everywhere. My mother, bless her soul, was converting to Judaism when she died, and I myself spent years studying Hebrew.

I became an attorney, practiced immigration law, traveled to Israel, voted Democrat, and engaged in protest marches. In short, I was raised as an SJW atheist and 'free-thinker' (read 'non-thinker') inside the PC Cult. At this point, therefore, having been 'reversed woke' by more recent events, I think I may legitimately claim to have some insight into matters relating to White Genocide, the Cultic nature of Political Correctness, its echo-chamber mentality, its predilection to censorship and violence, its incompatibility with the U.S. Constitution, and the participation of Unitarians and Jews in the Cult.

So, before dodging bombs hurled by ADL terrorists, and even though it's as certain as death in Texas that this little book will (again) be de-platformed at the urging of the SPLC, which specializes in the digital lynching of whites, and that I, despite my background as a lawyer engaged for years in promoting globalist activities and as a former SJW myself, will be dismissed as a 'racist' and doxxed and pilloried no matter what may reside between this book's covers – censorship, name-calling, and ad hominem attacks being as intrinsic to the Cult as breathing – I will point out that Jews and the PC Cult are not synonymous. Sorry to disappoint zealots on all sides, but my use of the term 'PC Cult' is *not* intended as code for Jews.

If the term 'PC Cult' seems vague given the absence of Cult membership cards, it is even harder to define 'Jew'. There are many who self-identify as Jews who regard themselves as conservatives or as nationalists in support of Israel or other nations, just as there are many people of Jewish ancestry who do not self-identify as Jews and who may or may not support the Democratic Party, or the Republican Party, or many other social or political entities. I have even known Jews who converted to Islam.

Generalizing always runs the risk of exaggeration, and Jews have many variants, from Central and East European Ashkenazi Jews, to Spanish and West European Sephardic Jews, to Mediterranean and North African Mizrahi Jews, and even Ethiopian and Indian Jews. Each of these sociological groups has its own distinct tradition and different political, or non-political, stances, making the age-old question as to whether Jews are a nation, a race, a religion, or merely a group of linguists nostalgic for a long-vanished past, more problematic than ever. I make no claim here that the PC Cult is a secret Jewish conspiracy such as is sometimes alleged to have convened in Salonika or in a Czech cemetery.

However, that aside, it is also true that while many self-identifying Jews support the Republican Party, many *more* self-identifying Jews – especially those most influential among other Jews – support the Democratic Party, which marches in lockstep with the Cult, and both wings of that partly-assimilated ethnicity known historically as Ashkenazi Jews remain united to a degree unknown to other self-identified ethnic groups in (1) belief in the sacredness of the Jewish Holocaust, and (2) advocating values that have the effect of harming non-Jewish whites everywhere they are implemented.

Whether these two positions imply supporting Israel or not, almost no self-identifying Jew of Ashkenazi background believes that the Holocaust should be allowed to be independently investigated or publicly questioned without the offender being subjected to social ostracism or legal prosecution. And in many countries to question any aspect of the official version of the Holocaust, for example asking whether six million Jews were killed or only 5,999,999, is a *crime* incurring mandatory jail time for Holocaust Denial. Even scholarly professors engaged in legitimate historical research can be jailed in some places merely for asking such questions.

For virtually all self-identifying American or European Jews, and especially those who support continued American financial and military support for the State of Israel, the Holocaust was "something *they did* to the Jews" and the removal of whites – as the 'they' in 'they did' – from power are the twin pillars that unite virtually all who self-identify as Jews, both Left-wing and Right-wing, these two causes being inseparable in their minds, even if they happen to donate to Republicans.

Why 'whites'? This conclusion may come as a surprise to the delicate reader, who perhaps feels no more personal responsibility for the Holocaust than he does for black slavery. The answer, as usual, lies in history. During the medieval period of alleged Jewish persecution, 'they' were the Christians, who, it is said, unfairly regarded Jews as 'killers of Christ'. When the age of religion vanished in the 19th century, 'they' in 'they did' became European nationalists and especially Russians, who tried to persuade Jews to assimilate. Finally, in the 1930s, 'they' became Nazis and Fascists, who had their own issues with Jews. But among Ashkenazis, the term Nazi did not *replace* European or Russian or Christian – the categories instead *merged* and became simply 'whites', which is the modern word for the ancient pejorative term 'goys', the gutter term for 'Gentiles', among allegedly secularized and free-thinking Jews.

Any public acknowledgment of the Jewish Holocaust today, therefore, in popular media and in academia has become code for the removal of whites because whites, Nazis, goys, Gentiles, and Christians have become inseparable, if they ever were separate, in the minds of most Ashkenazi Jews. Among hard-core Jewish SJWs, the terms Nazi, racist, fascist, Christian, Republican, goy, and Gentile, all mean exactly the same thing: *they are all code for 'white'*, and 'white' is the PC Cult's code word for any religious heretic who blasphemes the PC religion by refusing to accept his assigned status as a racial Untouchable.

But why would PC Cultists believe such nonsense? The source

of this terminological confusion among Cultists and so-called pro-
gressives and liberals, and the reason why these terms and epithets
have become so influential, is the Mass Media. American Jews of
Ashkenazi origin became entrenched in Hollywood over a century
ago. At that time, the word racism referred merely to an empirical
scientific theory that was popular in American and European colleges. White was little more than a descriptive term, and the word
Whiteness was totally meaningless. But after a century of relent-
less programming by the Jewish-controlled Marketing Machine,
white has become an insult, Whiteness an alleged pathological
condition, and racism religious blasphemy and a crime, with male
and masculine close runner-ups.

The only other ethnic group that can approach Ashkenazi Jews
in their self-conscious ethnic solidarity and in their refusal to
allow independent investigation of events that today form the ideological bedrock of their separate ethnic nationalism, is American
Blacks. Similar to Ashkenazi Jews when an outsider discusses the
Jewish Holocaust, Blacks respond with censorship and violence
to any attempt to treat Martin Luther King, or the Civil Rights
marches and the federal court-ordered desegregation movement
of the 1950s and 1960s, or the entire experience of black slavery,
as something other than eternally sacred totems. ('Black' denotes
a supporter of separatist Black Nationalism. Not all blacks are
Black.)

Jews prohibit criticism or investigation of 'their' Holocaust
with the same outrage and vehemence that Blacks prohibit criticism or independent investigation of 'their' Civil Rights Era and
desegregation and their 'African Holocaust' of black slavery, each

being the fundamental platform of their respective ethnic Nationalistic cohesion. And both are similar to Muslims who prohibit
criticism of Muhammad and discourage scholarly investigation
of the origins of Islam, which Arabs promote as 'their' national
religion even though most Muslims have not been Arabs for centuries.

The censorship of the PC Cult and its ad hominem attacks on
heretics casts a very long shadow. None of these groups has any
room in their brave new PC world for the existence of a white
population – keeping in mind that Ashkenazi Jews, although
mostly of European origin, absolutely, positively, heaven forbid,
do not consider themselves to be 'white', but 'black' Middle Eastern, even of pure sub-Saharan Black African, origin. I know it's
hard to believe – and Who ya gonna believe, them or your lyin'
eyes? But the prevailing view among tenured Jewish professors
in their imitation-since-ivory-is-banned Ivory League towers is
that there is no such thing as a Jew of European origin, but that
all Jews everywhere are 'black' *in the full biological sense* of
being genetic first cousins to sub-Saharan African blacks.

I refer the reader to tenured Jewish Professor Sander L. Gilman
of the Ivy League Johns Hopkins University. In his book 'Jewish
Self-Hatred,' he spells out in great detail this curious assertion
that Jews are first-cousins to blacks, and which must also come
as a surprise to geneticists the world over. Genetics aside, however, it all makes sense when one realizes that, for most Ashkenazi
Jews, white is the new 'goy', the 'they' as in '*they did* the Holocaust to us Jews'. So, of course, Gilman *must* insist that Jews are
biologically black or he would be faced with the prospect that

Jews are Europeans and did the Holocaust to themselves.

This explains how Goldman Sachs can comfortably refuse to deal with corporate Boards that consist of only white males. Goldman Sachs regards Jews as not white but black, therefore they can continue to issue IPOs where the Boards of Directors consist of only male Jews without violating their new rule. In Goldman Sachs-land, only whites who are not Jews fall into the new caste of Untouchables.

7
HOLLYWOOD

To say that Jews don't control Hollywood would be like saying Chinese don't control Beijing. In the 1970s, the actor Marlon Brando famously said that Jews control Hollywood and was roundly condemned for his 'anti-Semitism' and 'prejudice', which contributed to his moving to Tahiti. Years later the actor and director Mel Gibson made similar comments under the influence of a bit too much alcohol on a freeway shoulder and triggered a media storm that induced him to take refuge in Costa Rica.

They weren't Jews. In 2008, the Jewish journalist **Joel Stein** said *exactly the same thing* in an article for the Los Angeles Times (Dec 19, 2008) and was allowed not just to keep his job but to win awards and promotions. In his article, **Joel Stein** asked: "How Jewish is Hollywood?" His answer: "Jews totally run Hollywood." He pointed out that all the major media empires in the U.S. are owned or run by Jews (Jewish names **in bold**): recent NewsCorp President **Peter Chernin** (recall the allegedly 'conservative' NewsCorp owner Rupert Murdoch, who declaims to be a Jew though he had a Jewish mother); recent Paramount Pictures Chairman **Bob Iger**, who replaced **Michael Eisner**, and has recently returned to head Disney; recent Sony Pictures Chairman **Michael Lynton** (recall the alleged non-Cult nature of Sony, the 7th media powerhouse); recent Warner Bros. Chairman **Barry Meyer**; recent CBS CEO **Leslie Moonves** (whose great uncle was the first Prime Minister of Israel); recent MGM Chairman **Harry Sloan**; erstwhile NBC CEO **Jeff Zucker**; Screen Actors Guild President **Alan Rosenberg**; not to mention many more.

Stein wrote "Jews are so dominant, I had to scour the trades to come up with six Gentiles in high positions at entertainment companies. When I called them to talk about their incredible advancement, five of them refused to talk to me, apparently out of fear of insulting Jews. The sixth, AMC President **Charlie Collier**, turned out to be Jewish."

Keep in mind that 'goy' is the Jewish equivalent of calling blacks 'niggers'. Calling non-Jews 'Gentiles' is almost as bad as calling them 'goys', similar to calling blacks 'Negros' when one intends to show a lesser degree of disrespect than using the word 'nigger'. Using the word 'Gentile' is an ethnic insult when applied to whites. Stein knew this when he wrote his article.

Stein continued, "As a proud Jew, I want America to know about our accomplishment. Yes, we control Hollywood. . . I've taken it upon myself to re-convince America that Jews run Hollywood by launching a public relations campaign, because that's what we do best. . . I called ADL Chairman **Abe Foxman** [who] told me to my dismay, he was not hunting Nazis."

Recall that Nazi is code for white, having replaced Gentile and goy among allegedly secularized Cult members, and that most Jews insist they are *not* white. Hunting Nazis remains a popular Hollywood subject – witness its latest incarnation, the TV series *Hunters*, in which Jews hunt and gruesomely murder so-called Nazis in modern America, keeping in mind that among SJWs and many Jews the word Nazi means merely white. The TV series, therefore, is a thinly veiled call for the gruesome genocide of white Americans. Is it even conceivable that a movie could be released in the U.S. showing white Americans gruesomely killing Jews after the deliberate Israeli attack on the U.S.S Liberty which killed 34 American sailors and injured 174? Or showing whites gruesomely killing Communists who wear yarmulkas?

"He [Foxman] dismissed my whole proposition, saying that the number of people who think Jews run Hollywood is still too high." Curiously, as Jewish control of Hollywood has steadily grown, the public's perception that Jews control Hollywood has dropped dramatically, from 50% in 1960 to 29% today – this suggests that the 24/7 conditioning of the public by the Jewish-owned, Cult-directed Mass Media has been highly effective.

Stein continues: "The ADL poll, he [Foxman] pointed out, showed that 59% of Americans think Hollywood execs 'do not share the religious and moral values of most Americans,' and 43% think the entertainment industry is waging an organized campaign to 'weaken the influence of religious values in this country'."

Well, there's earth-shaking news. . . Need I do more than mention **Bill Maher** and his constant attacks on traditional religion? Yes, more: after a truckload of money-losing films that push anti-Christian soft porn agendas like *The Magdalene Sisters*, with yet another well-funded anti-Christian money-loser always coming just around the corner, Mel Gibson's self-produced, self-financed, pro-Christian *The Passion of the Christ* embarrassed Hollywood by making $383 million.

But Gibson remains *persona non grata*, while the power of Jews in Hollywood remains so great that actors and media people, like **Whoopi Goldberg** and **Geraldo Rivera**, continue to convert to Judaism in droves in order to boost their lucrative Hollywood careers. Stein saw no problem with Jewish domination of Hollywood. Still citing Abe Foxman: "This does not mean that Jews make pro-Jewish movies any more than [Jewish doctors] do pro-Jewish surgery."

That is an amazing statement given the avalanche of purely fictional, viciously anti-white Holocaust movies that Hollywood never tires of making, compared to the total absence of Holocaust-type movies about non-Jews, such as movies about the Armenian Holocaust, or the Ukrainian Holocaust, or movies about the Holocaust inflicted by the Allies on helpless German civilians after World War I, or the Holocaust inflicted by the Allies on German civilians (again) during and after World War II, or movies about the Holocaust that was inflicted on Chinese by Stalinist Chinese Communists, or movies about the Holocaust inflicted by the Cambodian Communists, or movies about the Holocaust of non-Jews in World War II German prison camps who likely died in greater numbers than did Jews, or Holocaust movies depicting the centuries-long role of slave trading by Sephardic Jews in the Mediterranean and Atlantic, or the Holocaust of the population of the American South inflicted by the 'scorched earth' tactics of General Sherman and in the Union prison camps where captured Confederate soldiers were deliberately starved. Nothing to see here. . .

Though I should add that Jewish Hollywood does crank out many African Holocaust movies about black slavery in America and white transportation of blacks from Africa to the American

South – all of which happily depict yet more gruesome murders of whites – although Hollywood never portrays the incomparably larger Muslim enslavement of blacks over 1400 years, which is still happening today in places like Mauretania and Libya. And Hollywood always omits the fact that ninety percent of blacks transported across the Atlantic went to Brazil or the Caribbean, while the American South accepted proportionally very few blacks while simultaneously granting more legal rights to black slaves than did any other location in the Western Hemisphere or the rest of the world.

Or that Jews per capita owned more black slaves in America than did Southern whites, and that Jews were more involved at least per capita than non-Jews in financing and directing the black slave trade across the Atlantic, including to Brazil and the Caribbean, being perhaps responsible for most of the trans-Atlantic traffic. Or that Massachusetts ship owners, including Jews, were instrumental in blocking efforts by Southern states in Congress to abolish the Atlantic slave trade for many years.

Or that the many ethnic *pogroms* and civil wars in Africa have resulted in the murder of many millions of innocents in the past half-century alone, amounting to multiple Holocausts by blacks against other blacks, not to mention the growing genocide of South African whites by South African blacks which includes boiling white children alive, just as American Indians often took pleasure in doing. Again, nothing to see here. . .

And maybe this is a good place to recall the role of the wealthy New York Jewish Sackler family in inventing and aggressively promoting OxyContin among working-class whites and thereby launching the opioid / suicide Modern Holocaust among the white working class, which has not encountered the least resistance or comment from ethnic doctors who wrote OxyContin prescriptions for *hundreds of millions* of those expensive, deadly, and hyper-addictive New York City-based, Sackler-produced little pills. The silence of the Marketing Machine on the many *real* issues that afflict the U.S., instead of Hollywood Holocaust made-up fantasies designed to depict Jews and Blacks as eternal victims pure as the driven snow, is deafening.

Stein summed up: "Maybe my life spent in a New Jersey-New York / Bay Area-L.A. pro-Semitic cocoon has left me naive. But I don't care if Americans think we're running the news media, Hollywood, Wall Street or the government. I just care that we get to keep running them."

Well, what can one add to that? Except a quote from the hedge-fund manipulator and unofficial Godfather of the PC Cult, **George Soros** (born **Gyorgy Schwartz**): "If I had tried to take social consequences into account. . . my profits would have been reduced." [**Horowitz**, *The Shadow Party*, 2006, p.97]

And another interesting quote, from Steve Sailer: "Back in Golden Age Hollywood, eight major studios were nepotistically run by Jewish moguls who hired their relatives and in-laws as executives, and the other studio was owned by Walt Disney, who nepotistically hired his relatives as executives. For decades now, a controversy has raged over whether Walt Disney was anti-Semitic. No comparable controversy exists over whether the other eight studios were anti-Gentilic. In fact, the term 'anti-Gentilic' doesn't even exist."

Of course, if it did exist, it would soon be eradicated, deep-sixed, and erased by the Jewish-run media giants that control what we see, what we hear, and what most people – especially SJWs – *think* they know. Supposedly independent sources of information are also being gradually closed off. Even the YMCA, for example, is now owned by Jews from New York.

Of course, Jews don't control all media, but their influence is huge. According to Forbes (6/1/2016), 15 billionaires own most of America's News Media. According to the size of their personal wealth (Jews **in bold**):

• **Michael Bloomberg**, owns financial news giant Bloomberg Media, *Business Week*, and was three- time mayor of New York City;

• Rupert Murdoch, chairman of NewsCorp, co-chairman of 21st Century Fox until sold to Disney;

• **Donald & Samuel 'Si' Newhouse**, own Advance Publications, which owns newspapers in 25 cities, *Conde Nast, Wired, Vanity Fair, The New Yorker, Vogue, Bride, Gentleman's Quarterly, Self, House & Garden*, 12 TV stations, 87 cable TV systems, and the entire Random House publishing empire;

• James Cox, owns *Atlanta Journal-Constitution*, 6 other newspapers, 14 TV stations, 1 local cable channel, 59 radio stations;

• Jeff Bezos, founder of Amazon, owns the ultra-liberal *The Washington Post*;

• John Henry, owns *The Boston Globe*, Red Sox baseball team;

- **Sheldon Adelson**, owned casinos in Las Vegas & China, and *The Las Vegas Review-Journal* (deceased 2021, succeeded by his U.S.-Israeli wife **Miriam Adelson**);
- Joe Mansueto, CEO of Morningstar, Inc., also owns *Fast Company;*
- **Mortimer Zuckerman**, owns real estate, *New York Daily News, U.S. News & World Report* which publishes influential rankings of Best Colleges;
- Peter Barbey, owned *The Village Voice* (now defunct), Reading Globe & Mitten Manufacturing Company (formerly Vanity Fair Silk Mills), and *The Reading Eagle;*
- Stanley Hubbard, CEO Hubbard Broadcasting with 13 TV stations affiliated with ABC and NBC, and 48 radio stations, and PodcastOne;
- Patrick Soon-Shion, owns pharmaceuticals, *The Los Angeles Times,* and *The Chicago Tribune*;
- Carlos Slim Helu, Mexican cell phone magnate, owns Telmex and America Movil, the two largest telecoms in Latin Amer ica, also owns the largest individual stake in the Jewish-run *The New York Times*: 17%;
- Warren Buffet, owns Berkshire Hathaway, which owns 70 daily newspapers (recently announced he is divesting them, as he recently divested his airline stocks);

In fact, Jewish influence is wildly disproportionate to their direct ownership of media. *The Jerusalem Post* listed famous and influential Jews world-wide. It is interesting to see how many Jews hold positions that are highly influential in the media or in institutions that depend on the media to promote their personal values:

- **Sergey Brin & Larry Page** (SJW founders of Google)
- **Dominique Strauss-Kahn** (SJW head of the International Monetary Fund, member of parliament for the Socialist Party)
- **David Axelrod** (Obama's top adviser, was political writer for *The Chicago Tribune*; founded AKP&D Message & Media)
- **Allen Dershowitz** (Harvard law professor, at 28 was the youngest in Harvard's history likely due to his being active 'down south' in the 1960s civil rights movement, i.e., a dyed-in-the-wool SJW and big supporter of Israel)
- **Elena Kagan** and **Ruth Bader Ginsburg** (the 2 most steadfast SJW members on the Supreme Court. Kagan was dean of Harvard Law School when the proportion of Jewish law professors there rose above 50%. Ginsburg died in 2020, was replaced by Justice Sotomayor who is of questionable religious background)
- **Irwin Cotler** (M.P. Canada, 'human rights activist', was Director of McGill Univsity's Human Rights Program, an expert in International and human rights law, i.e., another big SJW Cult member.)
- **Michael Bloomberg** (New York City mayor, got the 2-term law changed so he could serve a 3rd term, the 8th richest person in the U.S. During the Wuhan Virus he donated $40 million – *not* to white victims in the U.S., but to black victims in *Africa*, displaying classic SJW behavior of favoring non-Americans over Americans, and blacks over whites.)

- **Bernard Kouchner** (French Foreign Minister, founder of *Medecins Sans Frontiéres*, a prime Cult NGO that helps bring southerly migrants into Europe by any means possible)
- **Sheldon Adelson** (owned casinos, perhaps the biggest supporter of Israel and Netanyahu, owns *Yisrael Hayom*, the biggest Israeli paper, also owns Hebrew tabloids; succeeded by **Miriam Adelson**)
- **Mark Zuckerberg** (SJW founder of Facebook with 3 others, one of whom was **Dustin Moskovitz**)
- **Steve Ballmer** (billionaire former CEO of Microsoft)
- **Michael Steinhardt** (investor, together with Charles Bronfman sponsors the Birthright Israel program)
- **Mortimer Zuckerman** (owns *New York Daily News, U.S. News & World Report*, Boston Properties, and chairman of "Conference of Presidents of Major American Jewish Organizations")
- **Ronald Lauder** (Estée Lauder fortune, and President of the World Jewish Congress)
- **Larry Ellison** (founder of Oracle, the world's richest Jew, the 6th richest person in the world)
- **Elie Wiesel** (multi-millionaire, originator of the term 'the Holocaust' in reference to the Jewish experience in Germany during WWII), hs set up a wide network of Holocaust museums in white countries
- **Steven Spielberg** (a key PC Cult propagandist with productions such as *Schindler's List*; in cooperation with Elie Wiesel he established a Holocaust film and video archive)
- **Sir Jonathan Sacks** (Chief Rabbi in the UK and the British Commonwealth)

- **Jeff Zucker** (recent CEO of NBC Universal)
- **Leslie Moonves** (recent CEO of CBS, relative of **David Ben-Gurion,** first Prime Minister of Israel)
- **Bob Iger** (recent CEO of Disney)
- **Eric Cantor (a liberal, was the only Jewish Republican in** Congress, big on Israel)
- **Lee Rosenberg** (President of AIPAC, venture capital)
- **Richard Goldstone** (SJW appellate South African judge, became head of the UN Human Rights Council, board member of several NGOs pushing 'human rights' globally, including Human Rights Watch; trustee of Hebrew University in Jerusalem; big supporter of the militantly anti-white, pro-black ANC which currently governs South Africa).
- **Thomas Friedman** (author, *New York Times* journalist, sometimes hard on Israel but still promotes Cult values)
- **Haim Saban** (Israeli-American dual citizen, media mogul, and big Hillary and Israel supporter: "I'm a one-issue guy and my issue is Israel.")
- **Jeremy Ben-Ami** (Director of 'J Street', a left-wing, pro-Israel lobby that funds candidates for federal offices, or perhaps more importantly, funds the opponents of any candidate who fails to publicly endorse American support for Israel.)
- **Shari Arison** (owner of Bank Hapoalim, Israel's richest person and the richest woman in the Mid-East.)
- **Simone Veil** (French woman lawyer, big on Holocaust Memorials, President of European Parliament).
- **Irving Moskowitz** (real estate tycoon in Florida, gives prizes to Jewish West Bank settlers.)

- **Gill Marcus** (SJW woman governor of the South African Reserve Bank, big anti-white ANC activist).

- **Bernard-Henri Lévy** (SJW philosopher who claims that Jews should provide a unique moral voice in the world – a prime leader in the PC Cult.)

- **Bob Dylan** (wrote and sang "Blowin' in the Wind," the anthem of the 'human rights' movement).

- **Roman Abramovitch** (Russian oligarch in Britain, owns Millhouse LLC investments, owns Chelsea FC soccer club).

- **Sacha Baron Cohen** (British actor, big on de-platforming critics of Israel, i.e., a major SJW).

- **Lucian Freud** (artist, grandson of Sigmund, famous painter, his 'Benefits Supervisor Sleeping' painting sold for $33.6 million, a classic statement of Cult values because it implies that the poor are entitled to efficient provision of economic benefits by the state, and that the state is failing in this duty.)

- **Omri Casspi** (Israeli basketball player, the first in the NBA)

I might also add:

- **Charles 'Chuck' Schumer** (SJW senator from Massachusetts)

- **Bernie Sanders** (SJW multi-millionaire Senator from Vermont who has never worked in the private sector aside from a few youthful odd jobs but has spent most of his adult life working for the state. A former candidate for the Communist Trotskyite Socialist Workers Party, 'Bernie' has stated he wants to abolish all borders, even allowing in highly contagious travelers with the

Wuhan Virus. In 2022, he voted to send many billions in American arms to Ukraine).

• **Adam Schiff** (SJW Congressman from California, a Harvard Law grad 'machine' politician, Vegan, and Israeli dual citizen now serving his 10th term in Congress, heading the House Permanent Select Committee on Intelligence (!); he also serves on the House Appropriations Committee, and formerly served on the House Foreign Affairs Committee (!). He has never worked for a law firm but did serve very briefly as a U.S. Attorney.)

• **Barbara Boxer** (former SJW Congresswoman from California)

• **Diane Feinstein** (former SJW Congresswoman from California)

• **Jerrold 'Jerry' Nadler** (SJW Congressman from New York, Yeshiva-educated, another 'machine' politician and Israeli dual citizen. Heads the Congressional House Judiciary Committee (!). An undistinguished student, he was hired by an all-Jewish law firm. He was awarded his law degree even though he worked full-time for two years as an elected legislator in the New York Assembly instead of attending all his law classes. This reminds one of Armand Hammer, the son of a Jewish Russian immigrant to New York who was a fanatical supporter of the Bolsheviks and was awarded a degree in medicine in 1921 without attending medical classes or taking exams.)

• **Peter Kann** (Chairman & CEO of Dow Jones & Co, which owns *The Wall Street Journal*)

• **Joe Roth** (recent CEO Walt Disney Picture Group)

• **Peter Roth** (recent CEO of Warner Bros)

- **Steven Bornstein** (CEO ESPN)
- **Dan Shulman** (CEO PayPal)
- **Joel Klein** (Chairman of 'conservative' NewsCorp).
- **Michael Schulhof** (former President Sony Corp of America)
- **Michael Lynton** (President Sony Corp of America)
- **Alan Levine** (Chairman of Sony Pictures).
- **Ronald Perelman** (New World Entertainment)
- **Chris Wallace** (Fox News Anchor)
- **Avi Arad** (CEO Marvel Entertainment)
- **Bret Stephens** (*Wall Street Journal & New York Times*)
- **Jerry Bruckheimer** (TV and movie producer)
- **Barry Diller** (Chairman, IAC/InterActiveCorp & Expedia; former CEO of Paramount; former CEO of 'conservative' Fox, Inc.)
- **Ira Einhorn** (famous SJW 'community organizer' of the 1970s in Philadelphia, convicted in absentia of strangling his common-law wife)
- **Samuel Goldwyn** (Founder of Goldwyn Pictures, deceased)
- **Steve Golin** (Founder: Anonymous Content LLP; co-founder: Propaganda Films, which produced over one-third of all music videos in the U.S. in the 1980s.)
- **Bob Greenblatt** (Chairman of NBC Entertainment)
- **Brad Grey** (CEO Paramount Pictures)
- **Rob Reiner** (Co-founder: Castle Rock Entertainment)
- **David Rhodes** (former President CBS News)
- **Bob & Harvey Weinstein** (Founders of Miramax. Harvey

was convicted of multiple counts of sexual harassment, against *shikhsas*, i.e., 'goy' white women.)

- **Jeff Zucker** (recent SJW President of CNN Worldwide)
- **Rich Ross** (Group President of Discovery Channel, Animal Planet, Science Channel, Velocity)
- **George Sidney** (Co-Founder of Hanna-Barbera Productions)
- **Fred Silverman** (former President & CEO of NBC)
- **Larry Tanz** (Vice-President of Netflix, reputed nephew of the 1930s public relations propagandist **Edward Bernays**)
- **Dana Walden** (Co-Chairman & Co-CEO of Fox Broadcasting Co)
- **Mindy Grossman** (CEO Home Shopping Network)
- **Jonathan Klein** (Former President CNN)
- **Carl Laemmle** (Co-Founder of Universal Pictures. Deceased)
- **Noah Oppenheim** (President of NBC News)
- **Yoram Globus** (Israeli founder of Cannon Group, Inc., Founder: Rebel Way Entertainment)
- **William Fox** (Hungarian-born founder of Fox Film Corp. & DeLuxe)
- **Allen Ginsberg** (SJW 'poet laureate' of the PC Cult)
- **Bonnie Hammer** (Chairman: NBC Universal Cable)
- **Steven Hirsch** (Chairman, Vivid Entertainment, 'adult' content)
- **Brian Grazer** (TV and movie producer, Founder: Imagine Entertainment)
- **Jeffrey Katzenberg** (Movie producer; Founder: Dream-

Works; Chairman: Quibi)

- **Harvey Levin** (Producer, Founder of TMZ)
- **Mark Levin** (Libertarian writer & TV host, big Israel supporter)
- **Dave Rubin** (Libertarian TV host, big promoter of Israel)
- **Al Goldstein** (Founder of *Screw Magazine*)

Then there are the Hollywood Jewish comedians, who I am the first to admit are hilarious and beloved – but are often harshly critical of the U.S. and make a career of mocking white Gentile society. This trades on the tradition of Jewish *chutzpah*, i.e., making brazen and presumptuous demands while lying with a straight face. I stopped counting Jewish comedians after identifying one hundred and twenty.

The number of Jewish professors who make media appearances is also very great, far too great to list here.

Then we have the Neocons, perhaps better termed 'Ziocons' due to their unqualified enthusiastic support for Israel: **Richard Perle, Paul Wolfowitz, Douglas Feith, Michael Ledeen, Scooter Libby, Charles Krauthammer** (deceased), **Stephen Bryen, David Frum, Robert Kagan, Dov Zakheim, Henry Kissinger, Norman Podhoretz, Elliot Abrams, Daniel Pipes, Richard Pipes, Eliot Cohen, Bill Kristol, Irving Kristol, Max Boot, James Schlesinger**. This list too goes on and on. . .

Many more high-profile Jews can be found at *en.wikipedia .org/ wiki/List_of_Jewish_American_businesspeople*.

While being Jewish *per se* is not an issue, and I have no doubt that most or all Jews named herein are exceedingly talented and completely honest and I have no intent to defame any individual and I will gladly retract the labeling as a Jew of anyone who is in fact not a Jew. But it seems to me that awards and promotions in the hothouse of Hollywood parallels the kind of tribal nepotism that has served Jews well elsewhere. There is also an unfortunate tendency among influential Jews who own the online giants, like **Sergey Brin, Larry Ellison, Mark Zuckerberg**, and **Dan Shulman**, just to name a few, to uncritically accept the pernicious advice of the Jewish-run, Soros-funded SPLC and ADL, implementing without evidence the 'suggestions' of these entities to de-platform and censor targeted whites as part of larger anti-white hate campaigns launched by SJWs.

Accepting advice from the SPLC or the ADL (CEO **Jonathan Greenblatt**) is a manifestation of Jewish tribalism and any Jewish-owned entity that resists this is subjected to intense pressure to 'get back with the program' and re-institute anti-white policies. Unfortunately, Jewish Attorney General **Merrick Garland**, head of the Department of Justice, has now thrown open the DOJ to these same anti-white 'suggestions' from the Jewish SPLC and ADL, another clear example of illegal tribalism.

Let's next list all the billionaires in the U.S. over $10B, with Jews again **in bold**, recalling that it is difficult to identify Jews due to their tendency to change their names to something that sounds non-Jewish, so the proportion of billionaires who self-identify as Jews, despite their names, may be greater than appears. I include the following to demonstrate how many wealthy Jews are involved in media or finance. Keep in mind that Jews are no more than 2% of the population of the U.S., according to official census figures at least, and keeping in mind that, due to a religious injunction, Jews historically resist cooperating with a census.

Over $10 billion: Jeff Bezos, Bill Gates, Warren Buffett, **Mark Zuckerberg, Larry Ellison, Larry Page, Sergey Brin, Michael Bloomberg, Steve Ballmer**, Jim Walton, Alice Walton, Rob Walton, Charles Koch, Julia Koch, MacKenzie Bezos (ex-wife of Jeff Bezos), the late **Sheldon Adelson**, Michael Dell, Phil Knight, Lauren Powell Jobs, **Carl Icahn** (corporate raider, hedge fund manager, stakes in PayPal, Apple, Netflix, Lyft).

Under $10 billion: Jacqueline Mars, John Mars, Thomas Peterffy, **Len Blavatnik**, Elon Musk, **Ron Perelman, Dustin Moskovitz, Donald Bren, Leonard Lauder, Thomas Frist**, Elaine Marshall, Jim Simons, Lukas Walton, Rupert Murdoch, Harold Hamm, Ray Dalio, Eric Schmidt, Charlie Ergen, John Menard Jr., **Steve Schwarzman,** George Kaiser, **Steve Cohen, Micky Arison, Donald Newhouse**, Abby Johnson, **Phil Anschutz, Jan Koum**, Jim Goodnight, Charles Schwab, David Tepper, Donald Trump.

Under $4 billion: there are too many of these billionaires to list, but among them are **Bernie Marcus** (co-founder Home Depot), **Arthur Blank** (co-founder Home Depot), **George Soros, Leon Black, Steven Spielberg, Leonard Stern, Gwendolyn Sontheim Meyer, Ben Ackerman,** and **Sam Zell**.

Of the over 600 billionaires in the U.S., it is rumored that at least half, or over 300, are Jews. And that number is rising.

Some, like **George Soros, Bernie Marcus**, and **Arthur Blank**, although included in lists of the under-$4B category, I suspect are worth much more. Soros in particular is rumored to control up to one trillion dollars and admits to having given more than $7 billion to his propaganda entities. Soros is a major player in the Cult's Marketing Machine, the largest single funder of both the SPLC and the politicized 501(c)(3) foundation *Media Matters of America*, which Soros created for the purpose of suppressing the voices of dissidents.

501(c)(3) organizations are supposed to lose their tax-exempt status if they take a political position. Yet Media Matters, one of the most blatantly politically partisan of entities, mysteriously retains its tax-exempt status, as does the Unitarian-Universalist Church, which itself is so politicized that it recruited volunteers for Democrat election campaigns and for anti-Trump protest marches during Sunday services in 2016.

Before we leave the topic of Jews in high places – and the above only scratches the surface – their predominance surprising even me since *I was told nothing of these facts when I was raised inside the Cult. . .* among immigration lawyers, there is an 'Immigration Bible' that every immigration lawyer in the U.S. uses on almost a daily basis – I used it for years, as did every immigration lawyer I met. A Jewish lawyer in Florida, **Ira Kurzban**, publishes this legal resource book called, logically, *Kurzban's*. This massive annual 800-page volume, filled with minuscule text, contains every nuance of each relevant decision reported by every immigration and appeals court in the U.S. It currently costs $760 plus tax. It is so massive and detailed that it is clear that a large team of lawyers and legal assistants works around-the-clock, year-in and year-out, to compose this annual volume and keep it current as part of a concerted effort to maximize immigration into the

U.S.

The dedication that Jews as a cohesive group demonstrate in promoting this immigration, and the wealth that they invest in this project to the maximum extent humanly possible is astonishing, including distributing printed advertising in Central America and Mexico, and who knows where else, to encourage immigration to the U.S. and identifying beforehand those lawyers and organizations and sanctuary cities that will assist them in every way possible whether they choose to enter legally or illegally, even sometimes providing guides, buses, clothing, and consumables to assist immigrant caravans. One of my personal tasks as an immigration lawyer working for a large immigration law firm was to contact deportees in Mexico and attempt to persuade them to reapply for entry, *even if they did not want to return to the U.S.* Is it any wonder that even the briefest of pauses in enforcing border security along the southern U.S. results in an immediate flood of illegal immigrants?

This book is not about Jews, but about SJWs and the PC Cult. However, I have been forced to partially document the position of Jews in American life because – whether Left, Right, or Center – most Jews seem to subscribe to the PC Cult's agenda of enshrining Diversity and Equality as America's state religion, and not just in America, but throughout the world.

Following the example of Joel Stein, it is perhaps easier to identify those high-profile, influential Jews who do not adhere to Cult values – *as far as I can tell, there are few or none.* Even those Israelis who refuse to open Israel's borders to unlimited southerly immigration seem to be strong supporters of unrestricted southerly immigration into white countries.

Before I move on, I should include the latest wrinkle in economic domination by the 'One Percent', which, it should go without saying at this point, is largely if not mostly Jewish, acknowledging that even people who appear to be Gentile often turn out to be Jews who changed their name or masked their ancestry to disguise their origins and continuing loyalty to other Jews, which is so pervasive that it surprised even Joel Stein, who should know who is a Jew better than anyone.

I suspect that the One Percent, in the U.S. at least, got that way by a simple mechanism, exemplified by Michael Bloomberg. Of course, Bloomberg is a good and honest businessman, as are most Jews, and certainly every Jew named herein – that's not the issue. But in 2000 he was worth only $2 billion, while today, even after spending $1 billion on his spectacularly unsuccessful bid to grab the Democratic Presidential nomination in 2020, he is worth at least $70 billion. That's a $68 billion 'profit' in less than 20 years. Nice work if you can get it.

But the 'work' is a gift from the Federal Reserve System, which for the past forty years has been headed *exclusively* by Jews. The one exception is Jerome Powell, nominated by Trump – who was excoriated by leading Democrats for daring to nominate a non-Jew to this traditionally Jewish position – and whose policies have turned out to be indistinguishable from his predecessors.

For much of this time, the Fed has provided loans to public corporations for from zero to one percent interest, which the corporations then used – not to improve or expand their businesses or prepare for a rainy day like an epidemic, which would have been fulfilling their legal duty to their shareholders – *but to buy back their own company stock*. Given the fact that most CEOs of large public corporations today have compensation packages that are pegged to their company's stock price, this provides a built-in incentive to buy back their company stock using the free money loaned to them from the Fed even when the company is not making a profit or may be on the verge of bankruptcy.

This has disengaged stock prices from company earnings across the board and explains how the stock market can rise even when the economy worsens and earnings are hardly to be found. Thus the Fed uses fiat money, which is indirectly a surreptitious extraction of wealth from the American public, to effortlessly enrich the already richest people in the world, like Bloomberg and other wealthy Jews, who are no longer required to do *anything whatsoever* to receive this largesse falling from Fed-Heaven, this vast indirect looting of the public treasury and of the treasuries of future American generations – except to send Hannuka cards to their brethren who populate the top positions in the Federal Reserve beneath the Gentile figurehead, Powell.

A stock market decline and a new Depression – likely already begun – are being made inevitable by the Fed's vast subsidization of the One Percent, increasing social inequality beyond anything heretofore seen in the U.S. This emerging disaster will take years to recover from and will wreck the lives of millions. One can only wonder who first promoted the idea of stock buybacks as part of compensation packages, and what were their informal ties to the Federal Reserve and to globalist banks?

The Federal Reserve System is not a branch of government but is privately owned, and technically neither federal, nor a reserve of anything, nor even a bank – but rather a consortium of global investment firms deliberately set up beyond the jurisdiction of the President or Congress or the Supreme Court and *whose identity is secret by law.* Who in their right mind would allow the setting up of such an entity if they knew the power of tribal nepotism entrenched in global banks? One can only speculate.

So, in conclusion, does this mean that the author is an anti-Semite? Not at all, despite what appears on the surface at least to be a highly organized looting of America by the Tribe as easy as if they were herding cattle, as exemplified by the recent FTX crypto scandal with its many Jewish participants and ties to Democratic Party Jewish donors. I made many Jewish friends in the Unitarian Church and in the Hebrew classes I took, and of the many Jewish professors I had in college, two wrote me glowing reviews for graduate school, for whom I still retain great affection and admiration, though they are now deceased. And I have Jewish friends even today, whom I greatly respect. None of them are in the One Percent or are SJWs, however. For me, anyway – unlike mega-politicized SJWs who are always looking for the next micro-aggression to become outraged about – politics is not personal.

And I object to the term anti-Semite, anyway, on the grounds that Ashkenazi Jews are not Semites, but mostly East Europeans genetically and culturally, and therefore to be a true anti-Semite means to be anti-Arab. The author is not anti-Arab. But also not anti-Jew. The author is anti-PC Cult and only opposed to those

Jews who participate in the Cult or who push PC Cult values on the rest of the world, which admittedly and unfortunately, seems to be a vast majority of those Jews who are of Ashkenazi background.

I also respect some Israelis. So long as they are not dual citizens steering American foreign policy to support Israel, I have no issue with them. As an American, Israel is simply not my business. Or would not be if my tax money were not sent there by dual citizen Congressmen. Or should that be '*duel* citizen' to indicate the hostility that many dual citizen Israelis residing in the U.S. seem to have for non-Jewish Americans?

It is not necessary to be Jewish to be a hard-core Cult member. Lauren Powell Jobs, for example, inherited her billions from Steve Jobs. She runs something called the Emerson Collective social justice group (Ralph W. Emerson is a Saint Second-Class of the very Cultish and globalist MLK-worshipping Unitarian-Universalists), and she also founded 'College Track' to help black students. SJWs it seems *never* sponsor whites *qua* whites, but always rush to sponsor blacks *qua* blacks. And she owns Terravera Natural Foods Co. The word 'natural' is another key give-away for Cult membership – not genuine nature, of course, but the Cult's pretend 'Mother Nature' version.

Brian Roberts, Chairman & CEO of Comcast, is an even more enthusiastic Cult member: "Diversity has always been, and continues to be, an important part of our culture. . . [For 50 years] we have been committed to promoting and increasing diversity. . . Diversity and inclusion is not an initiative or program with an expiration date. It's the right thing to do. . ."

Recall that the Congresses which passed the Affirmative Action programs in the 1960s insisted that these preferences would eventually expire. Justice Sandra Day O'Connor wrote in 2006 in *Grutter v. Bollinger* that race preferences should expire within 25 years, which means no later than 2031. But don't hold your breath expecting the Cult-infested Supreme Court to keep its word any more than they can read plain English in the Constitution. Despite the recent reversal of *Roe v. Wade*, which only passed 5-4, they can't. And they won't, since all testing trends indicate that black college admission test scores are as far below non-black as ever.

Roberts' statement sums up the Cult credo from A to Z: anti-white here, there, and forever, as an unquestioned article of faith and universal morality enforced by law. Oops, I just learned that **Brian Roberts** is also Jewish, as is his wife. His grandfather was a Russian immigrant who, like **George Soros**, changed his name to disguise his Jewish background, one of the methods that Jews have used for centuries to conceal their allegiance and origins – and which clearly still works.

8
ACADEMIA

If Jews don't control all the media, or all Wall Street, or all international institutions, even if they do control all of Hollywood, how did Jews become so dominant in the Cult that it can be fairly said that Jewish academic professors are the 'priests' of the PC Cult? The answer is simple: (1) by using the Marketing Machine to clothe Jews in the moral superiority of victimhood despite being the wealthiest ethnic group in the world, despite often having an ideology of racial supremacism, and despite having had a long history of slave trading of both blacks and whites; (2) by attaining control of Ivy League colleges, leading to a dominant intellectual position in American education.

While Jews do not control academia to the same extent that they control Hollywood and the mass media, they do exercise a degree of influence far beyond their numbers. The numbers are impressive enough. What began as a small presence in American higher education before World War I erupted into a significant presence in Harvard and Yale in the 1920s. This was a result of court decisions that broke the previous ethnic quota system which had traditionally limited the number of Jews in the student body of these specifically Christian private colleges with specifically Christian private charters, thus enabling greater Jewish participation in their student bodies.

Jewish lawyers successfully argued that talent should be rewarded on an individual basis without regard for the ethnic background of the applicant, and although Jews were, and are probably still, no more than 2% of the U.S. population, by 1922 Jews already amounted to 20% of the student body at Harvard and have now surpassed 35%.

Two percent is an estimate. As mentioned, it is difficult to ascertain the exact number of Jews in the U.S. or elsewhere due to religious injunctions against Jews submitting to a census. Orthodox Jews in particular are notorious for evading censuses, taxation, and military service wherever they live, even in modern Israel.

This matched similar developments in Europe, where traditional quota systems in French and German universities broke down after 1900 under the pressure of Jewish litigation, Jewish book publishers, and editorial campaigns in Jewish-owned newspapers, resulting in disproportionate representation of Jews in European higher education.

The European intelligentsia were 'astonished' by the intellectual capacity of the many Ashkenazi Jewish migrants who left the over-populated Jewish areas of Tsarist Russia in the 19th century, making the familiar claim to be 'refugees', and Europeans realized that if Jews succeeded in breaking the quota system, their national universities would soon be swamped by Ashkenazi Jews of doubtful loyalty at the expense of their own people.

American universities were already in the throes of an intellectual revolution since 1900 under the impact of Jewish intellectuals and professors, such as **Sigmund Freud**, **Emile Durkheim** (his father was a rabbi), and **Max Weber**. Beginning with City

College of New York, the 'Harvard of the Proletariat', by 1930 Columbia University became the first Ivy League college in the U.S. to be preeminently Jewish in both students and professors, residing as it did in the midst of a swarm of Yiddish newspapers and journals in the city that had the largest Jewish population in the world. And the largest Jewish banks, thanks to such as the speculator Jay Gould, the Schiff banking family (Adam Schiff, head of today's Congressional Intelligence Committee, is a Schiff family relative), the Warburg banking family (lampooned as Daddy Warbucks of Little Orphan Annie fame), and the Rothschild banking family, among many other Jews involved in the centuries-old, primarily Ashkenazi occupations of lending, pawning, and finance.

In the 1920s, the writings of Karl Marx and Professor **Franz Boas** joined the above list of influential Jews. The 'New York Intellectuals' movement of Jewish literary figures that emerged in New York City in the 1920s was explicitly Marxist and Stalinist, and as the 1930s arrived, Yiddish gave way to English and their influence on American letters grew to dominate American publishing as they acquired control of New York book publishing companies, exerting a profound influence on American education.

From Vienna, Sigmund Freud's psychoanalysis was already taking the U.S. by storm in 1909, when Freud was invited to visit Clark College. After arriving, Freud decided he hated "matriarchal" America, where men "are led around by the nose" by women because women naturally develop faster in coeducational settings and this caused psychological harm to young men. Freud deplored the nation's "cultural state", declared that it was "a damage to civilization" and "a gigantic mistake", and he vowed never to return to the U.S.

Durkheim and Weber founded modern sociology. Both died before Jews achieved hegemony in New York City: Durkheim of a stroke in 1917; Weber of Spanish flu in 1920.

From Columbia, however, Professor Boas exerted a decisive influence over American Anthropology in the 1920s, and became notorious not only for his favoring Jewish students for promotion to professorships but in later years it was discovered that he had invented data for his own researches. He also sponsored Margaret Meade in her famous sojourn among the Samoan Islanders. Her work was also discovered in later years to have been invented or wildly distorted but approved by Boas due to her highly critical attitude towards American society in general and Christian sexual mores in particular.

This tradition of academic fraud among Jews continued into the 1980s with the Jewish Harvard professor **Stephen J. Gould's** book *The Mismeasure of Man*, which was also later shown to contain invented data and deliberately fraudulent assertions, which did not prevent him from joining the ranks of tenured Jewish professors, and whose text is still used today by SJW instructors at all levels of education although its fake scholarship was exposed years ago.

Boas fathered the first 'Revolution' in Anthropology, popularizing the notion of equality among all races and peoples. Equality, of course, was not a Jewish invention, but had been a core American value since the Revolution – understood within limits, however. The Founders had in mind primarily Lockean contractual 'equality' ("dickering over dobbin" in lawyer-speak) and equality of a middle class versus a landed aristocracy. By 1800, for example, all American states had prohibited European-style entailed estates, thus preventing the development of an American landed aristocracy. Entailed means intergenerational restrictions on alienation of landed estates. Ending entailments made land a commodity in the U.S., creating a market in land, the first country anywhere in the world to do this.

'All men are created equal' was in the Declaration of Independence but for good reason 'equality' was kept out of the Constitution since the Constitution had to be a practical and realistic document and there is nothing less realistic or practical than pie-in-the-sky notions of equality among people who are by nature very unequal.

Boas, however, advanced the notion, radical at the time even for revolutionary Jacobins, that all people the world over had exactly the same capabilities, including exactly the same intelligence, and that this equality would become apparent if only their cultural environments were made the same because in his view environment does not merely trump genetics – environment is all there is. To Boas, genetics is no more than a Blank Slate, and aside from physiology, has no influence on behavior. This became the discipline of Cultural Anthropology and these assumptions soon spread to other academic fields.

The Boasian view prevailed by the late 1930s, all scientific research on race and on physical and intellectual differences among different populations came not only to a halt – any researchers who attempted to investigate such topics afterward were subjected to such personal and professional pressure that they were forced to resign or abandon their research.

After World War II the rapidly expanding college system under the G.I. Bill led to an increased demand for PhDs, and the new Jewish-dominated Ivy League schools of Harvard, Yale, and Columbia, newly fleshed out with Jewish 'refugees' from Europe, met this demand by awarding PhDs like party favors to their Tribal graduate students.

The views of Boas, Freud, Weber, Durkheim, and Marx, and of the Frankfurt School of Jewish Marxist intellectuals: **Marcuse, Adorno, Lukács, Habermas, Fromm, Löwenthal, Pollock, Horkheimer**, et al, were heavily promoted by this cohort of newly minted Jewish professors, as were what later became the PC articles of faith: the Blank Slate, the presumed absolute equality of all persons (excepting the superior intellectual capacity of Ashkenazi Jews, which was never questioned), and the presumed moral superiority of Jewish matriarchy, which traces Jewishness through the female line (a genetic concept), versus 'fascistic' Christian patriarchy.

The Frankfurt School began in the 1920s as a Marxist research club of Jewish intellectuals in Frankfurt, Germany, but soon branched into Nietzsche-inspired Existentialism, paving the way for the later transition from Marx to Nietzsche in the U.S. In 1935, the Frankfurt School relocated to New York City and its leaders joined the teaching staff of Jewish-dominated Columbia University.

In 1950, the American Jewish Committee published Adorno's *The Authoritarian Personality*, a book devoid of scholarship, and which attempted to smear traditional Christian American families by setting up a stunningly inept 'F-scale' by which their psychiatric health was scored according to how allegedly 'Fascistic' they were on this 'F-scale'. This simple-minded book by a Communist Trotskyite Jew living in a Jewish enclave in wealthy Pacific Palisades, Los Angeles, soon became a standard text in Ivy League classes taught by other 'refugee' Jewish professors, alongside selections on Socialism by Karl Marx and philosophy texts by the Nietzsche-inspired Existentialists Heidegger and Sartre, and the recent popular philosophers **Karl Popper, Leo Strauss, and Jacques Derrida.**

Books such as The Great Gatsby, with its barely disguised denunciation of the American racialist researcher Lothrop Stoddard, and of Madison Grant who was an environmentalist and champion of white Europeans, became *de rigueur*. Grant was the chief proponent of Physical Anthropology, and not coincidentally, the chief professional rival of Franz Boas at the American Anthropological Association.

The Great Gatsby was part and parcel of this Jewish-controlled media assault on what had been a well-documented scientific tradition of empirical racial research by non-Jews. This situation still prevails in American academia, and under American pressure, has come to prevail in European universities. The continued promotion of Gatsby, a mediocre work originally reviewed as 'no more than a glorified anecdote', and 'a minor performance', was heavily pushed by the *New York Times* and by New York publishing executives during World War II, after the U.S., under strong pressure by Jewish intellectuals, had joined the Second World War as an ally of the brutal Communist dictator Stalin – not for the book's literary qualities, but for its anti-white propaganda value. This, and only this, explains its continued use in today's classrooms as part of the PC Cult's indoctrination, inevitably accompanied by its even more poorly written, anti-white PC twin, and largely fictional: *To Kill a Mockingbird*.

While Adorno and Co. were living in Pacific Palisades and Manhattan, non-Jewish professors and journalists with decades of publishing and doing original highly qualified research found themselves by 1950 shut out of higher education and no longer able to publish or teach. Preeminent scholars such as Harry Elmer Barnes, David Hoggan, and John Wear are virtually unknown today. Some, like Barnes, Henry Ford, and Charles Lindbergh, made the political error of joining the America First Committee before Pearl Harbor. Others were simply too critical of the Workers' Paradise, the Soviet Union, and of Stalin to be tolerated by the Bolshevized New York Jewish literary establishment.

This exclusion and censorship of once leading academics also continues today, with the expulsion or persecution of Professor Kevin MacDonald (*The Culture of Critique*), World War II historian David Irving (*The Bombing of Dresden*), and sociologist Charles Murray (*The Bell Curve*), and many others who have been blacklisted by PC academic departments. The Black historian Tony Martin, who researched the role of Jews in the slave trade, whose works the writer consulted for parts of this work, was subjected to such intense pressure that his last book before retiring was titled *The Jewish Onslaught*, which described the coordinated efforts by Jewish media and Jewish academics to have him silenced and fired. One may speculate that had Martin been white instead of black, he may not have survived in his teaching position, but would have been purged long before his formal retirement.

The recent explosion in knowledge of genetics and Human BioDiversity (HBD) has exposed the falsity of the Boasian view, but this has not stopped SJW professors, often but not always Jewish, from continuing to teach the Boasian Error and the Lewontin Fallacy (alluding to the debunked genetics theories of Professor **Richard Lewontin**) in their classrooms and banning outright any genetics research, joined by personal attacks on dissident researchers whenever possible.

The politics of personal destruction was known among Communists as 'Stalin's method' – it has since become standard operating procedure in today's PC Cult and its Antifa street militia, repeated when SJW Jewish Massachusetts Senator Charles 'Chuck' Schumer publicly threatened two Supreme Court Justices by name (Kavanaugh and Gorsuch), inviting assassination attempts on white conservatives by rank-and-file fanatical Cultists. When SJWs attempt to get people fired or when SJW hitmen attempt to assassinate Republican Congressmen or a Supreme Court Justice, this is the 'Stalinist method' in action – more SOP for SJWs and Communists.

It has often been observed, and is certainly true, that in academia science progresses one funeral at a time. And it is clear that the false values and pseudo-science of Boas, Gould, Gilman, Lewontin and the rest of the PC Cult will not finally be removed from academia until most professors over the age of 65 retire or die. Why 65? Because the peak of so-called 'liberal' influence in the U.S. occurred in the 1950s and 1960s when the current crop of tenured PC professors were students learning at the feet of professors like Boas, and they remain blissfully unaware that HBD research has passed them by. They still believe in the Marxist myth that environment trumps genetics and react with anger and censorship and ostracism and shouting down – the classic SJW media-conditioned responses that bypass rational thought – when forced to confront the fact that their 'knowledge' is obsolete. In fact, was never correct in the first place.

An average of 25% of the professors at all Ivy League colleges in the U.S. are Jewish, and over 50% of the professors at Harvard Law School. How did Jewish professors come to be so numerous? Yes, Jews are smart – but they're not that smart. Not 35% of the student body at Harvard and 50% of the faculty at Harvard Law School smart in a population of 330 million where they are only around 2%. Not when only 11% of students who achieve high enough grades to be admitted to the prestigious top-ranking fraternity of Phi Beta Kappa are Jews. The answer, whether among the club of Freudian psychoanalysts, or among Trotskyite Frankfurt School intellectuals, or among Ivy League professors in the post-World War II era, or among Hollywood executives is *tribal nepotism*.

For example, in his voluminous book that denounces what he calls Self-Hating Jews, Gilman cites only Jewish writers. His book turns out to be little more than an irrational attack on any Jew who displays independent thought that deviates in the slightest from Gilman's SJW values, which for Gilman includes first and foremost a slavish and blind loyalty to Israel. This from an American citizen teaching in an American university – who ought at least to give cognizance to Israel's deliberate attack on the American U.S.S Liberty in 1967, a failed false flag operation deliberately implemented at the highest level of the Israeli government and covered up by the very liberal U.S. President Johnson.

This is part of the secret of Jewish success in academia: every citation in a so-called 'peer reviewed' work like Gilman's chalks up brownie points for the cited author. Academic papers do the same thing by listing tens or as many as fifty authors for every published article, no matter how small or how minor, or how biased the publication. This is a great way to make undistinguished scholars appear to be brilliant and massively popular among other scholars and help them cross the finish line to tenure or to cover up false data.

It also helps if loyal Tribe members own the publications where an Associate Professor must publish to become a full Professor. Just as ending the death penalty only rewards criminal gangs and ultimately results in criminal inmates controlling the prisons, in academia, allowing Tribal nepotism pays big dividends and ultimately results in the Tribe running the universities.

Despite Gilman's odd insistence that the experience of Jews in American Ivy League universities has been, in his word, "horrific" (sic), due to the supposed rampant anti-Semitism that prevails, I think it more informative to note that the chances of a white Protestant male being accepted at Harvard today – although white Protestants are over half the nation's population, and their classroom scores qualify them to be up to 89% of Phi Beta Kappa, many multiples of the number of Jews who score that high – is almost as remote as bagging an elephant on the moon.

About as remote, in fact, as a Protestant obtaining a seat on the Supreme Court, which, if we disregard Gorsuch whose status as a Protestant is questionable, leaves only newly appointed Justice K.B. Jackson as the only Protestant on the Court since the days of Sandra Day O'Connor in the mid-1990s. And Jackson's Protestantism is not merely questionable – her true religion is the PC Cult.

It has been alleged that Justice Sonia Sotomayor, although formally Catholic, is Sephardic Jewish by ancestry, both her father's name 'Sotomayor' and her mother's maiden name 'Baez' common among Portuguese Sephardic Jews. Whether Sotomayor identifies as a Jew or not, she is certainly an SJW and votes solidly with Kagan and Jackson.

Justice Kagan, in fact, presided over Harvard Law School when it boosted its proportion of Jewish professors to over 50%, another text-book demonstration of Jewish tribal nepotism. This was where Jackson matriculated and when Obama was made head of the Harvard Law Review despite not having written a single article, which was without precedent. While formally not a dual citizen with Israel, Kagan is free to become an Israeli citizen any time she chooses since she is of clear Jewish descent, an option in fact open to all American Jews who can demonstrate that they are genetically of Jewish background, whether formally 'dual citizens' or not – perhaps even Sotomayor, given her enthusiastic support by *The Jerusalem Post*. ('Kagan' is the Russian spelling for the common Jewish name 'Cohen'). Jews no longer exercise their long-standing headlock on the Supreme Court, but its sole (officially) remaining Jewish member is joined reliably by SJWs Sotomayor and Jackson, with Roberts solidly 'on the fence'.

Then there are the multiple Jewish organizations. Light years beyond what exists in any other ethnic group, Jews band together to promote Jewish causes to an extent that is simply amazing, as if political and sociological mobilization were as natural to Ashkenazis as breathing, or as indispensable as circumcision and Seders.

Even their organizations are organized into organizations. The Anti-Defamation League; the Southern Poverty Law Center; the Conference of Presidents of Major American Jewish Organizations; B'nai B'rith; the Alliance of Black Jews; American Federation of Jews from Central Europe; American Jewish Historical Society; American-Israeli Cooperative Enterprise; the Ashkenaz Foundation; Asra Kadisha; Association for Jewish Outreach Programs; Call of the Shofar; Center for Initiatives in Jewish Education; Coalition on the Environment and Jewish Life; European Jewish Parliament; Lubavitch Youth Organization; Socialist Children Farband; Union of Italian Jewish Communities; Women's International Zionist Organization; Women's League for Israel; World Forum of Russian-Speaking Jewry; World Jewish Congress; Association of Israel Political Action Committee (AIPAC). . .

I'll stop there. Wikipedia lists over 65 pages of Jewish organizations. Almost by definition, a Jew who does not belong to multiple Jewish-only clubs and organizations that push the interests of Jews as Jews is not one. However, any white organization that attempts to push the interests of whites as whites is by law racist and illegal. There is no organization anywhere in the U.S. that may legally exclude Jews, blacks, women, or any so-called 'person of color'. However, no organization in the U.S. may legally call itself the 'Association for White Outreach Programs', and there can be no 'Union of White Students' or 'Union of European Students' in any college to promote the interests of white students of European ancestry – by law. Every organization of every stripe may nevertheless legally exclude whites, and especially males, which makes white males today's Untouchables in a Supreme Court-designed and implemented social system of Bubba Crow.

65 pages vs. Zero sounds to me a lot more like 'privileged Brahmins versus powerless caste of Untouchables' than it does 'poor refugee Holocaust survivors victimized by white privilege'. Conversely, the assistance which these Jewish organizations provide to Jews who seek advancement in finance, media, new online business ventures, or academia – often using public funds – cannot be overestimated. It goes far in explaining the emergence of a virtual Jewish aristocracy in today's West, and the Jewish 'priesthood' that continues to provide the moral values that inspire the globalist PC Cult.

The strangely prevalent American prejudice favoring individualistic Libertarianism also massively assists tribal-conscious Jews every step of the way. The ideology of 'Me, Myself, and I' Libertarianism is profoundly self-defeating because its hyper-individuality allows no provision for defending the integrity of American institutions under assault by highly cohesive tribes like Jews who act in concert (and not only Jews, though Jews do it best) and who raise nepotism to a high art form, steadily excluding non-tribe members and stealthily replacing them with members of their own tribe who have taken non-Jewish names or a new religion to disguise their infiltration, while indignantly denouncing 'Nazi Anti-Semitism' in the Jewish-owned Mass Media if their pro-tribe bias is ever revealed.

The disproportionate presence of Jews in academia and their near complete devotion to the PC Cult enables the awarding of numerous PhDs to aspiring members of the Cult in subjects such as: Systems Studies (code for Diversity indoctrination); Gender History; (Anti-) Whiteness Studies; Feminist Economics; and ethnic Studies programs that champion every ethnicity conceivable – except white or European. All of these so-called degrees are actually 'divinity degrees' awarded by tax-subsidized, tax-exempt PC seminaries that teach the Cult's Religion of Diversity. They are not certificates of mastering bodies of knowledge as colleges are supposed to teach, and as the public assumes, but acknowledgments of full membership in the PC Cult, certifying the student acolyte's admission to 'priesthood' status, issued by tenured priests in the Cult's academic 'mosques' for having proved their adherence to the Cult's politicized Party Line.

Acquiring knowledge is only incidental to this proof of 'PC Communion', and college examinations in these subjects are co-incidental or not administered at all, the ritual of participating in a protest march or escorting busloads of southerly illegal immigrants to a Sanctuary City, functioning as a de facto, tax-supported criminal cartel, is sometimes the only requirement to complete these college classes, with top grades assigned based on the student's 'Wokeness' or success in violating federal and state law.

Indeed, this is what lies behind the current trend of dropping college entrance exams like the SAT. The new criterion for admission to Ivy League colleges is not intelligence or grades, but 'Wokeness'. Intelligence or prior academic accomplishment only interferes with producing the Cult's next generation of fanatical, anti-democratic SJWs, who can attain entrance to these colleges with any level of IQ – or without demonstrating any intellectual ability at all. A high IQ would only interfere with the indoctrinatin.

As with so much of PC Cult activities, the nation-wide censorship by Jewish-controlled media of virtually all avenues of information that reach the American public ensures that the public at large will remain asleep in a media-induced coma and will never hear about this takeover of American educational institutions.

Investigate the background of one's college professors and the texts they teach and one may discover that not only are one's professors Jews, but the texts they teach were written by Jews, that the publishers of the texts are Jews, and that the citations to which the texts refer will cite still other texts that were written by still other Jews. And, if the texts or videos are provided online – which today they always are – the internet services which deliver them will be owned by Jews, starting with Google, ensuring that the students will never see anything in their entire 'educational' career that might contradict the Cult's carefully selected or invented 'facts'.

Even if the names of the CEOs do not appear to be Jewish, research often reveals them to be self-identifying Jews who changed their names. Even a DNA test may not reveal the truth because the leading company, 23AndMe, is owned by the Jewish wife of one of the Jewish owners of Google, having every incentive to obscure inconvenient test results, or mischaracterize them as national as opposed to racial categories, just as Google obscures inconvenient news, maintaining the Jew Taboo with the help of the SPLC's censorship and physical threats from the ADL or from masked Antifa goon squads to deal with individuals who remain uncooperative even after they have been censored, de-platformed, and de-banked.

Jewish professors, therefore, being the intellectual core of the Stalinist / Trotskyite coastal elites since at least the 1950s, and using their well-rehearsed tribal nepotistic techniques brought from Europe, today constitute the 'priesthood' of the PC Cult, and alone of all ethnic groups can never be criticized in the Main Stream Media. Criticizing Jews on any popular website is the surest way to get shadow-banned or de-platformed with even one's credit cards and bank account canceled. Not even the NAACP can do that. (Like the SPLC, the NAACP was also founded and is run by Jews, not by blacks.)

Control of the media and targeted censorship by Jewish-owned New York book publishers such as Simon & Schuster and Random House assist in this tribal occupation by imposing a near total news blackout on their successful waging of tribal warfare and Talmudic 'pilpul' lawfare to implement this systematic exclusion of whites from countries that whites built. And by implanting in the minds of the public at large the odd notion that it is immoral to listen to facts that might show Jews in a negative light or might reveal their take-over of American media and academia, and that a good SJW must reject such facts, and refuse to listen to the 'evil Nazis' who point out such facts and attack its source in a fit of violent moral outrage.

By these methods, Jewish dominance of American media and academia today has become so extensive that it is difficult to watch any putative informational or academic discussion on cable or YouTube without discovering that both sides in the alleged debate are dual citizen Jews, both sides always in full agreement that the biggest danger to the U.S. is, ironically, not Jewish racism or Jewish Supremacism, but a moribund White racism and White Supremacism.

Donning the cloak of pretend science, the PC priesthood pontificate from their taxpayer-financed Ivy League towers, pushing the entire litmus of topics calculated to provoke brainwashed SJWs into responding with outrage and violence to any perceived challenge to the Cult, whether to Jewish institutional dominance or to the moral values of the PC Cult. Secure in their tenured positions for life – just like the Cult members on the Supreme Court are tenured for life – the Ivy League priesthood denounce whiteness and whites, maleness and males, hurling 'Nazi', 'racist', 'fascist' and 'KKK' (but never 'JKK') at anyone who dares question their right to use American tax money to corrupt American institutions in furtherance of their fanatically anti-American and globalist, Trotskyite-inspired, fanatical PC religion.

9
ORIGINS OF THE CULT

Despite its dominance among the New York Intellectuals, Marxism was never just a Jewish 'secular' movement. Marxism was led by Jews, and Jews adopted it as their chief ideology everywhere they went as their rationale for resisting assimilation to host national cultures and retaining an international Jewish culture, Israel being 'the only nation without borders' as Disraeli put it. *But the rank-and-file Marxists were not Jews.* Rather they were ex-Christians who no longer wished to identify with any formal religion, often making the claim that Marxism was the logical fulfillment of the Enlightenment, and that they therefore were secular 'free-thinkers', meaning free of religious dogma.

This was wishful-thinking. There is no such thing as humans without myth, or 'free-thinkers' without religion, or true atheists despite what they claim. Marxism was not secular at all, but was itself a religion, every bit as fanatical and anti-rational and violent as anything that preceded it in the Age of Religious Wars. Marxism was neither secular Judaism, nor the fulfillment of the Enlightenment, but was the revenge of a defunct Catholicism and a declining Calvinism against the Enlightenment.

Most Marxists were ex-Christians. They were frustrated Templars who had lost faith in the Temple. They were Crusaders looking for a new Jerusalem to storm. They were secular Jesuits eager to combat a secular Satan. They were disillusioned Pilgrims who still clung to the values of a discarded Christianity complete with self-sacrifice, an imminent Heaven on Earth, brutal suppression of heretics, a stridently anti-democratic dictatorship of believers, and a fierce excommunication of any who dared question their right to wield absolute moralistic power. But, contrary to Christianity, Marxists were led by Jews unleashed from, or involuntarily dragged out of, their ghettos by the French Revolution and eager to seek bloody vengeance on goys for perceived centuries of abuse, happy to use a deceptive Marxism as their tool for controlling the 'useful idiots' of the ex-Christian rank-and-file.

This leadership of European Jews over European Socialist thought – and Marxian thought was the only socialist thought that mattered – had its climax with the Russian Revolution. Ashkenazi Jews constituted over 80% of the Bolshevik leadership and seized power in an armed coup eight months *after* the Revolution. It can be fairly said that if Marxism was secularized Christianity, Communism was secularized Judaism. The Jews' messianic impulse led them to search out and worship a strong Dictator-Messiah: first Lenin, who was at least one-quarter Jewish by blood and another quarter Kalmyk-Mongol, then either Trotsky or Stalin.

Russian Jews favored Stalin even though he distrusted Jews and purged most from the Party leadership and murdered them during the Purges of the late 1930s. A few Jews in the West began to break with Stalin in the 1920s in favor of Trotsky. But the exiled Trotsky was murdered in Mexico in August 1940 by one of Stalin's assassins. (The assassin was awarded the Hero of the Soviet Union medal in Moscow after his release from a Mexican prison twenty years later).

Why this lesson in the history of Marxism? Because Marxism – first in its incarnation as a European Jewish intellectual movement, and then in its Communist Trotskyite version – was the predecessor of today's PC Cult. Both were globalist movements nurtured and led by European Ashkenazi Jews, and both today's tenured Jewish priesthood in America's Ivy League universities and today's leading Jewish Neocon / Ziocon Republican-leaning intellectuals are the children of former Jewish Trotskyites, called red-diaper babies, who sought to preserve the globalist nature of Marxian Communism from Stalin's barbed-wire Soviet borders and to pursue their quest to abolish the borders of all European nations and America.

Like the PC Cult, Communism promoted radical equality, but unlike the Cult, Communism had little interest in race relations. Communism was all about socio-economic class. Race relations only became an important part of the Soviet Union's Party Line when it became clear in the 1950s that, despite decades of energetic propaganda, no Communist working-class movement would ever emerge in the United States. Marxism just did not speak to Americans.

But a different philosopher did: one who spoke clearly and directly to Americans, and whose ideas were the very antithesis of Marxism – Friedrich Nietzsche.

In the 1950s, Marxism increasingly gathered dust, but the ideas of Nietzsche flooded America. Leftists like the Frankfurt School spent less and less energy discussing class war and armed revolution and instead began to speak a new and different language, discussing Authenticity, being true to oneself, psychiatry, the irreducibility of feelings, the importance of fundamental values, and how to cope with an unknowable existence which coping became known as Existentialism. TV's **Dr. Ruth** and sex therapy proved far more interesting to young Americans than Marx or Trotsky.

By 1969 Marxism in the U.S. had become a ghost. One can see this by visiting any major library and looking at the circulation evidence on the inside back cover of books about the Soviet Union and Marxist theory – circulation slowed through the 1960s and practically ceased after 1969. As of 1969, International Communism was dead. Nietzsche, an insane German proto-Nazi philosopher from the 1880s, posthumously put a stake through the heart of Communism – just as Hitler's invasion of the Soviet Union in 1941 eventually proved fatal to the Soviet Union, though long delayed.

Communist ideologues did their best to keep up. In terms of ideology, the 'missing proletariat' went through many incarnations as Party ideologues in Moscow experimented – as far back as 1919 they substituted various groups for their missing proletariat: herders, peasants, miners, saintly exploited owners of a single cow as opposed to evil exploiter 'kulaks' who owned two cows, etc. In the 1950s, as Communists worriedly searched for some group that might substitute for America's missing proletariat and keep the sagging cause of Communism alive in the United States – and Stalinists and Trotskyites who competed for the allegiance of their mostly upper and middle-class East Coast Jewish supporters – Communist ideologues moved down the scale of income and education in their search for an allegedly unfairly exploited, over-worked, and under-paid economic group in the U.S.

The new proletariat, which in Communist theory was expected to mushroom in size until finally seizing power in a glorious bloody revolution, became: truck drivers, day laborers, or fruit-pickers. Communists wanted a group who were smart enough to organize but not so literate that they might reject the leadership of the Party. None of the above proved suitable. Finally, by the early 1960s, the Party had a formula that seemed to work: blacks in the American South. Without any formal announcement, embracing blacks meant that class conflict was jettisoned and was replaced by race relations since race is not class, but cuts across classes. With this move, Communists embraced the stake that Nietzsche had thrust through the heart of Marxism.

But that wasn't the end. By 1970, a whole new crop of left-leaning intellectuals began using the language of Marxism to press their own very Nietzschean (i.e., non-class and very self-focused) political agendas. Seeing how successful American blacks had been in getting the Black Agenda adopted by the Supreme Court and Congress – with the help of impressive but legally irrelevant *amicus curiae* papers written by Jewish professors – resulting in race-based Affirmative Action, other groups hurried to join the Victimization Queue for Free Stuff.

Whites in general, frustrated by the free ride that blacks got in the 1960s, pushed their wives to the forefront, discovering suddenly in the 1970s that women were an Exploited Class, as true a 'proletariat' as blacks, and therefore deserving of the same privileges and the same Affirmative Action, although women as a group cut across class lines even more starkly than blacks.

Middle-class housewives, formerly scorned by the Left as spoiled beneficiaries of pampered bourgeois life, fled their middle-class houses by the million, rushing to enjoy a new Affirmative Action of their own, receiving promotions despite little work experience because, after all – they too were victims of unfair, age-old discrimination. This gave them one up on blacks, because no sooner did blacks begin to enjoy their government-dictated promotions over white males than white females did an end-run and were promoted ahead of both – the same white females who were married to the same white males who, just a few scant years earlier, had been the blacks' evil bosses.

Suddenly blacks, despite their Affirmative Action, by 1980 found themselves subjected to supervisory boards composed *entirely of white SJW females* and wondering how the heck that had happened. This writer has personally witnessed the bitterness and outrage of blacks when encountering a government panel composed exclusively of white women officers, and the smugness of the white SJW women in response. White SJW women, it seems, are just as capable of tribal nepotism as anyone else.

Then the Queue got even longer. More and more groups got in the Victimization Line: teachers, air traffic controllers, public service employees, Hispanics, Indians, Chinese, Pakistanis, Gypsies, Pacific Islanders, Gays, Transsexuals, college professors. Even Ivy League grad students like Hillary Clinton and Elizabeth Warren, people who in former times had been universally considered the most privileged and wealthy elite in the history of the Universe, all joined the ranks of Social Justice Warriors claiming to be victimized minorities demanding their Affirmative Action, even when they were numerically by far the majority of the nation's population.

In time absolutely every identifiable ethnic or economic group, no matter how minuscule, even extinct ones like Hawaiians and Mohicans, joined the gravy train and were duly rewarded by the SJWs sitting on the Supreme Court, who found ever more 'Fundamental Rights' hiding invisibly in the Constitution to support these eager groups with their faux anger and clenched fists, who played the role of victim to the hilt. SJWs *are always victims*, even when they put down their Frappucino milkshakes and double-park their Ferraris in their Harvard Faculty parking spots so they can punch a white male 'Nazi' plumber in the face. They then sue the plumber for harassing their fist.

Each new group was duly recognized – provided that it excluded white males, or if white males were unfortunately already among the group, provided that white males remain a class of Untouchables within the group, tolerated only so long as they show a willingness to publicly beat their breasts in shame, and willingly sacrifice themselves on the new SJW altar of Diversity.

Groups that formerly insisted they were white began to reject that label and insist that they were anything but 'white': Mexicans, Cubans, Mulattos, Arabs, Turks, Persians, Macedonians, even Italians from Italy and Spaniards from Spain, who had been 'white' for as long as the word existed, discovered suddenly that their barely detectable tans made them 'black' and that they too were therefore victims of age-old discrimination at the hands of melanin-deficient evil white males who always hailed from somewhere further north.

And males with less than average testosterone, who formerly had been accepted by all as true men, if not particularly manly, began to reject the label 'male' and insist that they were 'women trapped in a man's body' and sought surgery to correct 'nature's mistake'. They too put on the SJW cloak, and as angry victims, demanded their share of Supreme Court enforced quotas and Affirmative Action along with unrestricted bathroom access enforced in every establishment across the country, regardless of its effect on children and the rest of society.

Even the disabled got in on the act, though in their case they were more numerous and the discrimination more genuine – but the Supreme Court limited the enforceability of the Americans with Disabilities Act within a short time after it was passed by Congress, with the explanation that it was 'time to close the door on creating more Fundamental Rights in the Constitution,' showing their readiness to continue legislating from the bench in direct opposition to clear Congressional intent. Even for the Cult members on the Supreme Court, granting rights to the disabled was a bridge too far. Unless, of course, the disabled also possess melanin or ovaries – then they qualify for limited promotions via Intersectionality. But if they lack melanin or ovaries, then Whiteness cancels out the Wheelchair, and as white males, they and their wheelchairs were pushed out of the Victimization Queue and back into the ranks of white male Untouchables – a new subcategory of Untouchables within the Untouchables.

Soon, therefore, so many had fled the label 'white man', anxious not to be tossed into the new caste of Untouchables, that it seemed there would be none left anywhere in the world save a single albino in his wheelchair, a Dr. Evil plotting to destroy the World with his evil twisted Whiteness from a secret cave near the North Pole, the one person left who had neither melanin nor ovaries to redeem him, and therefore was responsible for all the world's racism, sexism, and every other -ism.

Stated more accurately, though: the only person left who had no tribal representative on the Supreme Court to secure his narrow interests at the expense of the rest of society. This was made clear by the appearance of melanin-absent albinos and melanin-deficient red-heads as the villains-of-choice in Hollywood movies (2006 *The Da Vinci Code* and 1976 *Dune* respectively), and by the growing lethal mob attacks on albinos in Africa and the street murders of 'gingers' in London by lynch mobs of dark-haired SJWs playing at Captain Planet.

Thus, to their surprise, former Communists found themselves in the 1980s at the forefront of a huge hydra-headed movement of discontent that was not only splitting the U.S. apart, but as America's chief export, was spreading across the globe with every exported movie and every faux college degree conferred by profit-worshipping colleges on visiting foreign students in exchange for *mucho dinero*. This vast Victimization movement became known as Political Correctness, first named as near as the author can tell in a cartoon series in *The Daily Texan*, drawn by Berke Breathed, as a modern restatement of the old Communist Party Line. Already in the 1970s, his ultra-liberal cartoon characters were asserting that people should be 'politically correct' by calling teenage girls 'pre-women' instead of 'teenage girls'.

Sometimes Communists, frustrated and feeling left behind by

these very un-Marxian developments, tried to take credit for this PC movement. See, for example, the videos by the former Soviet intelligence agent, Yuri Bezmenov, who tried to claim credit for this highly successful undermining of the West. But in truth Nietzsche was more responsible than the Kremlin in birthing it. Today's PC Cult is far more Nietzschean than it is Cultural Marxist. We could call it 'Cultural Nietzscheanism' and some call it Post-Modernism, but 'PC Cult' makes more sense and is easier to spell.

So Marxism is gone and has been replaced by Nietzsche, just as class conflict is gone and has been replaced by race conflict, the former supreme social evil in the 1930s of 'red-baiting', a term that was roundly hated at the time by Leftists, suddenly enthusiastically embraced by today's Left now that it has become 'white-baiting'.

Although still run by Jews, just as Marxism had been, today's PC Cult is no longer Communist but has become a golem, a self-perpetuating mindless cultural vacuum that was created by Jewish red-diaper babies and by Jewish-owned Hollywood, using the international mass market propaganda machine that was fashioned and run by Jewish Communists in the 1920s in the service of Stalin and the Soviet Union. Communism – the God that failed – has long gone, but the golem lurches today along the same track, devoid of guidance from either Trotsky or Stalin, but still slouching towards a messianic Frankist-porno Jerusalem, fomenting race riots and STDs and abortions and a Luddite anti-science irrationality everywhere the golem stumbles.

The PC golem now lives and breathes on its own, blessed by

senile pre-Boomer Trotskyite Jews like **Bernie Sanders** and **Noam Chomsky** who still rail against the Marshall Plan as a Capitalist Plot, and clumsily directed by a loose conglomerate of Trotskyite Jewish billionaires like **George Soros, Tom Steyer, Seth Klarman, Haim Saban, Ben Ackerman**, and the multi-billionaire **Pritzker** and **Sackler** clans ($14 billion and counting among the twenty pill-happy Sackler members), among many others, who are the chief donors of today's profoundly undemocratic Democratic Party, and who decide which candidates will be backed by the DNC and which will be ignored and left behind as roadkill, like poor deluded Moscow Bernie.

These donors are the lifeblood of the PC Cult. First and foremost: the walking mummy who thinks he's God, George Soros: "To put it bluntly, I fancied myself as some kind of god. . . I carried some rather potent messianic fantasies with me from childhood." Soros' latest campaign is to fund SJW district attorneys in county elections across the U.S. with the purpose of nullifying law enforcement, which has had dramatic results – in many large cities local D.A.'s are now often canceling bail for blacks arrested for violent crimes and BLM riots, and putting them back on the street with only ankle bracelets. This is having the predictable result of black criminals simply wearing their ankle bracelets when they commit more crimes, there being not enough supervisory personnel in the world to keep track of so many bracelets.

1 0
MAIN FACETS OF THE CULT

FREE SPEECH

One of the peculiarities of the Cult is a perception, deriving from Nietzsche, that there is no such thing as objectivity. Beginning with Kant and developed by Hegel, both Marx and Nietzsche, from opposite political orientations, attacked the notion of independent objectively verifiable facts. Marx proclaimed that individual consciousness was determined by class consciousness, with the individual's ideas and outlook and values entirely formed by that individual's class.

Nietzsche insisted that if objective facts exist at all, they are either unknowable or are useless to humans, consciousness and so-called Free Will being nothing more than unpredictable and obscure physiological processes. As the chief proponents of Marxism in Europe, Ashkenazi Jews used their ownership of Europe's leading newspapers to popularize Marxism, while absorbing Nietzsche's ideas in the background by osmosis.

When Jews came to America, they brought both Marx and Nietzsche with them, teaching that free will did not exist and that objectivity was impossible and that therefore professors should no longer aspire to intellectual independence but should embrace their prejudices and be proud of them.

This is how speech became 'violence' in the minds of SJWs.

Because if truth does not exist – only prejudice – then discussion is no longer a way to discover truth, but merely a deceptive way of disguising one's bias and bigotry, subtly exercising privilege and power over others. Thus, the PC Cult's focus on 'safe spaces' where speech-as-violence (not to be confused with violent speech) is banned and the evil heretics who commit speech-as-violence by the 'micro-aggression' of opening their mouths and stating their opinions are silenced, excommunicated, and expelled.

And this is also why voting is *per se* illegitimate in the eyes of SJWs. Voting, after all, is only a form of speech, so voting is also nothing more than a deceptive way of disguising the speaker's hate and prejudice and his exercise of illegitimate power and must also be suppressed. SJWs do not elect their leaders by majority vote – they are chosen by 'Intersectionality', which means measuring candidates by their degree of melanin and non-heterosexual-maleness. The only 'communicating' that SJWs do is with baseball bats and their preferred 'voting' is to stuff fake absentee ballots into unsupervised boxes at 3:00 A.M.

The election of Congressmen and -women, who might commit the cardinal sin of compromising PC Cult values once they arrive in Congress, is no more acceptable to SJWs and their Intersectional Cult than would be popular election of their professorial priesthood in the hierarchy of academia, or popular election of the Cult's representatives on the Supreme Court. To SJWs, *popular elections are by their nature sinful because they violate the sacred principles of Diversity and Intersectionality*. Therefore, free and open elections must be avoided whenever possible.

If forced to participate in a majority-vote election, SJWs believe the results should be rigged as happened in 2020 and more routinely in places like California. And if forced to accept the actual results of a majority-vote election – but losing – then the results should be *canceled* by the Cult's backstop SJW judges in the federal judiciary on the pretext that the results were unconstitutional, i.e., violated Diversity and Intersectionality by 'suppressing the vote' of some unidentified 'people of color'.

Just as any Orders issued by a President who was elected in an election that the Cult's candidate lost to must be resisted or ignored. PC values *always* trump majority-vote elections, including any executive branch orders that may follow such elections. The PC Cult accepts the results of votes and of any other legalistic governmental processes established by the Constitution *only if they win*. They then celebrate the 'triumph of Our Democracy' and the 'restoration of our Constitution' that had been 'threatened' by evil white males – but only as an exercise in public relations. Like with the SJW Hillary Clinton in 2016, the duty to abide by the results of an election applies only to heretics and Untouchables, never to SJWs themselves.

This is called Cancel Culture. In its narrow version, Cancel Culture is the suppression of blasphemy by so-called 'private' but in actuality quasi-governmental corporations functioning as an Inquisitional arm that persecutes heretics on behalf of the government's state religion. In its broad version, Cancel Culture is the globalist Cult acting as a state within the state. The Deep State has been thoroughly infiltrated by Cult members. The struggle against the Deep State, with its Five Eyes secret relationships among corresponding Cult members in other countries of the Anglosphere, not to mention the intelligence services of Saudi Arabia and Pakistan – where the dual citizen Awan Brothers kept backup servers retaining classified damaging information on up to forty Democrat members of Congress – has become a struggle to restore national sovereignty and the true Constitution against the globalist, anti-national, omnipresent PC theocracy and its unconstitutional, bizarre, logic-twisting principles.

If SJWs further consolidate their power, we can expect them eventually to call for making each person's voting choices a matter of public record, allegedly in the interest of transparency, but actually to intimidate people into voting 'correctly'. This is part of what is behind the call for ever more mail-in ballots. Mail-in ballots can not only be faked. Every ballot can also be indefinitely preserved. Then the signatures, among the genuine ballots at least, can be leaked to the public in the interest of transparency, or leaks threatened for future political blackmail for having once voted against the Cult.

It never seems to occur to SJWs that subjectivity might be like bacteria. Sure, bacteria are everywhere and it's difficult to create an environment free of them. But just because it's difficult to create sterile conditions doesn't mean surgeons should perform their surgeries in a sewer. With their enthusiastic embracing of subjectivity, SJWs are celebrating performing surgeries in sewers and demanding that everyone else do the same – or else.

'NATURE'

The strange thing about the PC Cult's view of nature is that, although SJWs pretend to worship it, they in fact do the opposite. They do everything they can to violate, ignore, contravene, or modify nature. They embrace 'natural', but they pierce, tattoo, shave, abort, implant, and bend genders at every opportunity. They want to 'save the planet', but they condone environment-destroying high birth rates by blacks. They ban plastic bags, but buy environment-polluting plastic computers by the million. They call for preservation of American wilderness, then rush to help illegal immigrants devastate border states with their waste. They cry for world peace, but happily subsidize ethnic wars in the Congo by buying cell phones constructed with Congo's conflict-mineral coltan. They want to save polar bears, but scream with outrage when someone proposes saving the children of coal miners in Appalachia. They condemn birth control among Africans, but insist on government-subsidized abortion among whites. They champion the indigenous outside of Europe, but enthusiastically genocide indigenous Europeans. They promote tribalism among their favored ethnicities, but condemn tribalism among disfavored whites. They praise polygamy among dark Arabs, but angrily prosecute polygamy among white Mormons.

They promote gay marriage as something natural, but embrace unnatural late-term abortion and post-birth murder. They preach social control over the individual as part of nature, but in the same breath insist that women should be able to unilaterally abort without regard for abortion's destructive effects on husbands, fathers, community, or the nation as a whole – not to mention the death of the aborted child. They preach back-to-nature and conservation, but invite in millions of baby-popping migrants who can't spell 'nature' or 'conservation' to save their lives, and who will never join a conservation society or visit a national park in their entire lives – even if it's free. They call for abolishing borders and ICE and the Border Patrol, but live behind high walls and locked doors and employ hordes of private security to protect themselves in their gated neighborhoods.

They fall into a panic at the thought of global warming, but think nothing of flying to Paris for lunch in a private jet, and they never ride crime-ridden mass transit like *hoi polloi*. They champion biological evolution among animals and carefully document their rapid adaptation to local environments in periods as short as a century, but insist that there is only one human race that is exactly the same everywhere and which they claim has not changed in the slightest across multiple environments for 50,000 years – a scientific impossibility. They happily debate which dog breeds are the most violent or most intelligent or most loyal, but yell with outrage when biologists point out that human populations exhibit similar differences in violence and IQ and law-abidingness wherever they may reside and regardless of local environment and history.

The PC values of Diversity and Inclusion have implications far beyond what the Mass Media will allow to be discussed. These values imply that it is immoral to favor genetic similarity. Instead, one is expected to favor genetic *dissimilarity*. This is contrary to observed behavior in any species ever studied by scientists. The logical end of Diversity is not peaceful coexistence with everyone singing "Imagine" or "Kumbaya" over a campfire. The logical terminus is the destruction of the nuclear family since the family is the furtherance of one's own genetics. A country, after all, is a family writ large; abolishing the border is therefore the equivalent of taking the door off your house and announcing to the world that you don't care about your own offspring so everyone is welcome to move in, displace your children, and rob you blind.

Countries that protect their racial rural base – the source of its biological continuity – prosper and grow. Countries that adopt a so-called 'civic nationalism', i.e., inviting large numbers of hostile foreigners inside its gates, do not prosper. They suffer a permanent decline in living standards, confidence, trust, and respect for institutions, while crime and corruption and civil conflict skyrocket. Just as advanced countries grow under protectionism but decline under 'libertarian' free trade, white populations prosper behind strong borders that permit little non-white immigration but collapse under open borders with massive non-white immigration.

When a Nigerian immigrant or MS-13 gang member can walk into your house and demand the same financial, emotional, and economic benefits that you have provided to your own children at great sacrifice and expense, *that* is the next step in Diversity. That is happening today in Sweden, where a Muslim Pakistani migrant, Qaisar Mahmood, has been appointed head of the Swedish National Heritage Board, as the chief steward of Swedish culture and archaeology – which he and his Swedish colleagues have declared does not exist, *that there is no Swedish culture*. A surprising statement to anthropologists the world over, who must be amazed that for the first time ever a society has been discovered that has no culture.

The next to last step in Diversity is to demand that families be entirely abolished, that children be removed from their parents and put in state facilities run by people not genetically related to them. One may be certain that such policies will be enforced only among white families since in societies run by the Cult only whites are Untouchables and only white society has no culture. This discrepancy will be explained as a 'temporary' and 'prophylactic' measure to prevent the emergence of the ultimate evil of 'racism', recalling that, in the PC Cult view, only whites can be racist.

The last step, however, as explained above, is not more half-measures, but the complete eradication of whites, with their 'removal' to. . . well, what's the difference between a state facility where only white children go in and a state facility where no one comes out? Since there are no societies where whites are sovereign remaining anywhere in the world today outside of East Europe and Russia, and Russia is under perpetual warlike siege from the Cult-run United States, greatly amplified by the Ukraine conflict, whites can expect nothing for their children but one-way train trips to Inclusion-land under signs that proclaim 'Diversity Makes You Free'.

The PC view of nature is also peculiarly feminine, just as the Cult as a whole is peculiarly feminine in its psychology. The Planet is always Mother Earth. The Earth is always being 'raped', just as women on college campuses are always being 'raped' by evil white males, even if the college resides next to a mostly black district and crime statistics show that it's immigrant males or black college students or black males coming onto campus from the adjoining district who are doing any actual raping – it is noteworthy that there was never a problem with rape on any American campus until black males and immigrants began enrolling in significant numbers.

To find answers to these strange PC notions, one must look behind the facts to the Cult's religious myths and ideology: Christians allegedly persecuted Jews because they killed Christ. The PC Cult has turned this on its head: *the Cult persecutes whites because they killed Mother Earth*. In their view, the Earth has already died. A white cross is on its gravestone. The 'twelve years' of the Doomsday Clock when the Earth will finally flood or burn or otherwise expire under the onslaught of white male real estate developers and white male oil-drillers has passed and the Earth Mother has expired. But, like Old Testament women weeping over the dead nature-god Tammuz, we can reverse this result. We can rally to get the dead heart of Mother Earth beating again – if we can only get evil white males, with their sharp angular mathematics and their masculine penchant for facts and logic, and their masculine eating of meat, to vanish in a time machine back to the 1950s, so the sacred Earth Mother can revive.

Meat-eating, as something integral to maleness, is also something that allegedly harms Mother Earth. Except that it doesn't. A recent TED talk deviated from the usual PC nonsense that TED talks usually spiel by reporting a surprising discovery. For the past several decades, it has been a core article of faith among SJWs that global warming is to a large extent caused by too many cattle and overgrazed land. To save Mother Earth from the lethal effects of the masculine activity of eating meat, it is therefore necessary to get rid of cattle and for everyone to become vegetarians. In PCworld, even cats and dogs must give up eating meat and lie down with the lamb.

After a lifetime of wildlife management in Africa, however, conservationist Allan Savory found the exact opposite is true. The problem that is causing desiccation and erosion of topsoil in Africa and contributing massive amounts of CO_2 to the atmosphere is not too many animals, but too few.

It turns out that running large herds of herbivorous animals on packed desiccated soil quickly returns the soil to a profusion of vegetation that secures the soil in place, halting erosion and removing CO_2 from the atmosphere. The trick is to keep the cattle moving; they should stay in place only long enough to fertilize the soil with their waste matter and break up the soil with their hooves, then move on to greener fields. This can be accomplished by introducing a few predators or human herders to keep them moving. By cycling a large herd of cattle in a circle of near desert, the desert transforms into a lush grassland that benefits climate rather than harms it. But, to make this work, *people must eat meat.* That's the payback for their labor invested in preserving and cycling the cattle. If they are replacing natural predators, then people must harvest and eat the cattle to control their numbers.

But this interferes with the PC agenda of relieving their self-hating white guilt by helping millions of 'refugees' flee their homes which they themselves helped turn into desert by killing off their herds of wildlife and the natural predators; of having something like meat-eating to beat men over the head with; of having an ongoing global climate crisis for SJWs to endlessly complain about and demand unlimited political power to solve while they vent their Greta-esque outrage and drama. They would then have no more pretext for the Cult's Green New Deal, which would be exposed as nothing more than a disguised racial redistribution scheme taking from people who excel at creating wealth to those who only consume it, yet another extorted transfer payment disguised as social welfare to appease criminals, haters, rioters, and arsonists.

SOCIAL CONSTRUCTS

Following the precepts of Nietzsche, today's college humanities programs apply a process called Deconstruction. Formally, Deconstruction to SJWs is an exciting way to expose prejudices that dead white males allegedly inserted into their texts. However, Deconstruction is a way of breaking down every assertion, every claim, every social organizing principle, and ultimately all the social values or glue that hold together the institutions necessary to keep a society alive and functioning.

Nietzsche pioneered Deconstruction. Applying the acid of his psychological insight, he dismantled every value of 19th century Europe, showing, he believed, that Western Society was long past its prime and had entered into a prolonged decline, both intellectual and physiological, a decline he called Decadence.

While there is much to commend in Nietzsche's trenchant analysis of modern society and Christianity, and his predictions for the disasters of the 20th century were remarkably accurate, he unfortunately did not give the same guidance on how Decadence would finally reverse and what the new glorious society growing out of the ruins of Decadence would look like. He only claimed that an 'Overman' would appear at the right time with a new set of quasi-religious values and put Humanity back on track by founding a new civilization with a new set of positive values.

Nietzsche did not see this as racial, but implied that improved physiology would be part of this, and he praised Nordic 'blond beasts', leading critics to lampoon his 'Overman' as a racial Nordic 'Superman', although 'Overman' simply meant 'one who leaps ahead', and 'blond beast' may have been only a metaphor for lions. It is hard to say, though, since even Nietzsche's metaphors had metaphors and his works, like Nostradamus, were deliberately vague, so he may indeed have meant that Nordics were in some way biologically superior. Nietzsche, clearly (to this writer at least) sliding into insanity long before his final diagnosis, at times seemed to see himself as an Overman, a new Napoleon or Muhammad, but he admitted he was too ill and too early, that Decadence had to run its full destructive course before a true superior 'Zarathustra' could emerge and take control, maybe in the 22nd century.

Reluctant to give the 'Nazi' Nietzsche credit for inspiring their movement, the PC Cult still trumpets the names of dead Jewish males like Marx and Trotsky and Gramsci. But SJWs took Nietzsche's technique of Deconstruction and ran with it, Freud and Heidegger having led the way. Then they took the next logical step. Once everything has been deconstructed, any attempt to reconstruct must, by definition, be equally invalid, a mere Social Construct. This asserts – given the SJW assumption that environment always trumps genetics (which Nietzsche did not believe) –

that nothing is final, nothing is rooted, that the slate is always blank at birth, a tabula rasa, and that society can change anything it likes about human nature at any time in any way, if only the evil 'patriarchy' or 'capitalism' of white males would stand aside and oblige SJWs by conveniently dying. Therefore, although sex is predetermined, gender is something assigned by white male patriarchal society, a 'social construct', something that can be changed at will. And, although skin color is predetermined, race is also a concept allegedly invented by capitalist society, another social construct that can be safely ignored and easily reassigned.

But what happens when someone tries to 'reassign' his or her race? Recently a Jewish Congressman attempted to join the Congressional Black Caucus in the House of Representatives. After all, just as with the SPLC, Jews launched the NAACP and virtually all executives in both organizations have been Jews ever since, and the source of their funding has always been Jews, though the rank-and-file are often American blacks. Jews have always regarded blacks as natural allies in their 'struggle' against whites so it makes sense for them to ignore the restrictive social constructs of racist 'capitalists' and seek unity with blacks. . . But the answer from the Black Caucus was a resounding *NO*. As in Nyet, Nein, and No-way José.

For the entire fifty years of its existence, the Congressional Black Caucus has refused membership to anyone who cannot prove biological ancestry from sub-Saharan Africa. That's right: *race* – not skin color. Recently in Oregon, a young white woman named Rachel Dolezol, whose white SJW parents raised her with several adopted black siblings, did all she could to make herself appear Black (recall that capital 'B' means having Black Nationalist consciousness), and she rose to formal head of the local NAACP in Spokane. But when national Black figures heard that a white woman in Oregon was pretending to be Black, Rachel Dolezol was challenged and expelled. Apparently, being black is more than just skin color after all – even to Blacks.

It's okay for a white to darken his skin and write a book called *Black Like Me* if it's just a temporary sojourn to reinforce the Black permanent reservation in the Endless Victimization Queue. But don't think you have a one-way ticket. Because Blacks know that race is real and biological, and that Affirmative Action is not about leveling playing fields between whites and blacks, or even about achieving equal outcomes, but about securing a permanent advantage, which Blacks don't want to share even with their Jewish patrons. In the end, the Jewish Congressman seeking entry was just another Jewish Al Jolson putting on blackface to horn in and he was not welcome on their gravy train. The Caucus, in fact, are so race-conscious that they even deny entry to (gasp) Arabs, Spanish, and Italians, not giving a damn about their 'black' Mediterranean tans, and 'Black' Jews are no more welcome in the Caucus than 'Black' Irish.

And Jews are no exception. In 2016, the State of Israel passed a law restricting immigration to those Jews who can prove Jewish descent by DNA test – in other words, underlining the racial basis of Judaism, in opposition to classifications of Jews as an ethnicity or a religion or a linguistic fan club. As early as 1910, Freud wrote: "[I] belong to an alien race. . . [Jesus was] born from the superior Jewish race. . . I am, as you know, cured of the last shred of my predilection for the Aryan cause, and would like to take it that if [the Jewish Messiah] turned out to be a boy he will develop into a stalwart Zionist. He or she must be dark in any case, no more towheads. Let us banish all these will-o'-the-wisps!"

Towheads are people with blond hair. So 'will-o'-the-wisps' meant white Europeans, making this quote a barely disguised call for white genocide by one of the most prominent Jews of modern times. Though a few Sub-Saharan Africans still reside in Israel, the gate was shut to more Jewish African immigrants years ago and those who arrived are now being encouraged to depart. Blacks are no more welcome in today's Israel than Jewish Congressmen are welcome in the Congressional Black Caucus.

So just how 'real' is race? There is lots of evidence that race is not a social construct and cannot be separated from deeper biology. Countless studies show that SSAs (Sub-Saharan Africans) have local-environment-specific traits.

For example, West Africans have sickle-cell partial immunity to malaria. Other immunities to malaria have developed around the globe, but only West Africans have the sickle-cell version. Sickle-cell enables them to survive in malarial areas but also can make them very ill. West Africans also produce the fastest sprinters in the world. Not the most enduring, but the fastest short-distance sprinters, due to a special adaptation in muscle fiber integrity, which also comes in handy playing American football, basketball, and boxing.

SSAs are more likely than Europeans to have twins. Africans also sweat the most oil intermixed with water. East Asians, on the other hand, sweat almost pure water, with virtually no oil. Europeans are in between. And East Asians almost never have twins. Africans have ear wax that is oily; East Asians have ear wax that is comparatively dry. Europeans again are in between. These are only a few of dozens of very well documented racial differences, which are so much deeper than skin-deep that physical anthropologists can distinguish at a glance the skull of an African from the skull of a European, and the skull of an East Asian from both, which would be impossible if race were not real. An Artificial Intelligence program recently detected racial differences in X-rays, seeing traits that remain invisible to human researchers.

Despite the fantasies of SJW Critical Race Theory, which is nothing more than Deconstruction dignified by a fancy name, mountains of research have demonstrated conclusively that SSAs have an average IQ of around 70; Europeans 100 (set as default for math, verbal, and spatial-visual); American blacks around 85 (midway between SSAs and Europeans); Australian Aborigines around 65; East Asians 103-105; and Ashkenazi Jews around 112. The last is the highest average IQ of any ethnicity, but is only for math and verbal – Jews score half a standard deviation *lower* than the European average of 100 in spatial-visual ability. Spatial-visual skills are essential for physics and engineering but irrelevant for money lending or reading the Talmud. These differences all reflect the particular evolutionary pressures exerted by local environments over thousands of years. In fact, there is evidence that a group's average IQ can change dramatically in as little as 500 years. According to Gregory Cochran & Henry Harpending, Ashkenazi Jews may have gained their superior IQs in language and math only since the year 1400. (Cochran & Harpending, *The*

10,000 Year Explosion, 2009. For this and data below also see Nicholas Wade, *A Troublesome Inheritance*, 2015; and Edward Dutton, *Making Sense of Race*, 2020.)

There is also evidence that the IQ of Ashkenazi Jews is tied to the specific genetic ailments that a majority of Ashkenazi Jews suffer from: sphingolipid storage disorders (Gaucher's disease, Tay-Sachs, Niemann-Pick, and mucolipidosis type IV); disorders of DNA repair (breast cancer BRCA1 and BRCA2, Fanconi anemia type C, and Bloom syndrome); and as many as a dozen other Ashkenazi Jew specific genetic ailments, such as Canavan disease, and dysautonomia.

Israel has established extensive health programs to attempt to treat these many Ashkenazi-specific ailments, and a few Sephardic, which have resulted from centuries of special breeding patterns among Jewish communities in Eastern Europe. The Amish and several other small populations around the world also show a high incidence of specific genetic disorders, presumably for similar reasons of isolation and peculiar breeding customs, but only the genetic diseases of Ashkenazi Jews show enhanced IQ.

In fact, several Jewish genetic illnesses have been correlated to particular types of intelligence, for example Gaucher's seems especially to boost IQ in math and verbal ability. The Ashkenazi disease of torsion dystonia appears to result in an unusually high degree of intelligence, averaging 121 IQ. Jews with torsion dystonia are eleven times more likely than other Jews to work in highly intellectually demanding occupations. Ashkenazi Jews with these brain-boosting diseases are so common that they boost the overall average IQ of Jews to at least 112 although many

Ashkenazi Jews are no smarter than the average European – and most Jews are substantially *less intelligent* than the average European or American in spatial-visual ability, which perhaps explains why there are so few Jewish engineers.

Mizrahi Jews, on the other hand, average an IQ of only 90, like other North Africans and Arabs. Mizrahis also do not suffer from the smorgasbord of genetic ailments that afflict most Ashkenazis, presumably because Mizrahis lived in much larger numbers in the Islamic world for the past thousand years and never became pigeon-holed in money lending and Talmud-study in tiny self-isolated communities.

If that is not enough to 'cancel' the Cult's wrong assumptions about human equality and fungibility, it is well established that the higher rates of obesity and alcoholism among blacks in America and among Amerindians compared to whites are due to the fact that whites have a much longer history of agriculture in their genetic background, which enables whites to tolerate 'junk food' high in carbohydrates to a much greater extent than can blacks and Amerindians. The latter societies have practiced agriculture for a much shorter period of time, no more than 3,000 years compared to over 10,000 years for whites.

This is why obesity and diabetes in the U.S. are concentrated in areas with the largest populations of blacks, Hispanics, and Amerindians. Indeed, having white skin is probably one of the adaptations of a comparatively low-nutrition and high-carb diet that was brought about by agriculture in the cloudy climate of Northern Europe. Variable colored eyes are likewise products of this diet in this climate.

People with dark eyes and dark skin tended to die from mal-nutrition in clouded Northern Europe, and equatorial immigrants in Scandinavia today suffer from malnutrition for the same reason and must take vitamins to stay healthy. Indo-Europeans also adapted to consuming milk products in historical times and thus have no ill effects from lactose, while Amerindians and East Asians and most blacks remain lactose intolerant. Cattle-breeding Nilotics in Africa are an exception, but even this is comparatively recent historically. None of these differentials can be easily ex-plained by social environment alone without resort to long-stand-ing genetic adaptation in specific geographic locales.

SJWs, of course, living as they do in their giant Mass Media echo chamber – the six media giants acting essentially as a single monopoly – *know absolutely nothing about these studies* and uni-formly react with disbelief, outrage, and violence when brought to their attention. So don't try this at home, kids. SJWs don't give apples to their instructors, but send bombs in the mail like the Un-abomber, **Ted Kaczynski** – yet another Luddite SJW.

In today's colleges, SJWs refuse to condone research into race IQ, asking: "What purpose could such research serve except to promote white supremacism?" We just reviewed some very good purposes as regards race-related medical issues, which can be ex-tended to organ replacement and blood transfusions. The rejection of racial research is the same response that scientists like Galileo and Copernicus met when they gazed through the first telescopes and hypothesized that the Earth revolves around the Sun instead of the reverse. Every revelation that surfaces from biology depart-ments regarding race realism and every new investigation of human biological diversity is met with Cult attempts to halt the research, censor the results, physically attack the researchers, or get them fired for doing their jobs as scientists.

This clearly shows the anti-science nature of the PC Cult. Their attitude is a repeat of the Church's condemnation of Galileo requiring him to state that the Sun revolves around the Earth and forcing him on pain of death to repudiate his scientific discoveries. This happened recently with the DNA discoverer James Watson, who was forced to recant his statement that "all our social policies are based on the fact that [Africans'] intelligence is the same as ours – whereas all the testing says not really," a simple statement of fact that everyone but blindered SJWs freely acknowledge.

But just as applying ever more fanciful epicycles to planetary movements in desperate attempts to explain the planets' intricate movements in support of their false belief that the Sun revolves around the Earth led to the principle of Occam's Razor, a fundamental principle of scientific method that helped bring Europe out of the stagnant Middle Ages, SJWs' desperate search for 'systemic racism and sexism' to explain the continued glaring differences between blacks and whites and men and women should also be analyzed under Occam's Razor.

Today's PC Cult is thrusting the world into a new Dark Age and has instituted another Spanish Inquisition to stamp out facts and science, their 'racial epicycles' in the air being employed to explain their false assumption that white heretics are casting evil spells that mysteriously 'hold blacks down' or are somehow giving blacks the Evil Eye which makes it 'exhausting to be black'. Occam's Razor, however, says the problem isn't in the air, or in evil spells, but in blacks' genetics. And that there really is no problem at all – only a reluctance by SJWs to embrace the fact that there exist several easily identifiable human races and two distinct human genders and that these are *not* the same and cannot be made the same by *any* human effort short of centuries of eugenics or recombinant DNA which is currently beyond the capacity of human societies.

Even slow-witted SJWs at some level intuitively grasp these facts. Like Jessie Jackson, they too will hesitate to walk unarmed down a city's Martin Luther King Boulevard at night. They know that blacks are at least thirty times more likely than whites to commit a violent crime and far more likely to commit rape. They too, if given a choice between having a child with a demonstrated IQ of 60 or an IQ of 160, and not given the option of aborting them, will. . . well, is there really any doubt which child the SJW would select? We know the answer. We don't need piles of propaganda *amica curiae* from Jewish professors 'embracing their bias', or weather reports from Bob Dylan, or Reichian analysis, or dusty class war explanations, or it's-all-whitey's-fault Critical Race Theory. The SJW would of course choose the child with the demonstrated IQ of 160 in which to invest a lifetime of money, time, and energy.

And the SJW would then bribe the entrance counselor to get the child into Harvard. SJWs always seek to enter the most prestigious colleges that they can get into, and they are willing to pay, or have their parents pay, any level of tuition so they can attend and get that coveted Ivy League diploma. Ivy League colleges today are no longer about getting a liberal arts education or acquiring a job skill, but about climbing the social status ladder so SJW kids will get into the upper class and not end up working in tattoo parlors wondering whatever happened to Moscow Bernie's Revolution.

SJWs social climb better than anyone. They know that their only ticket to avoid their kid having to compete with white-hating migrants in 'fully diverse' workplaces after the 'No Whites Allowed' sign goes up is to secure free college tuition for their white SJW kid. If students want to take Feminist Psychoanalysis or Ethiopian Basket-Weaving for free (is there really a difference in PC-land?), maybe they should get their degrees in Venezuela or Cuba instead of the U.S.

On the gender front, we see the same thing. Transsexuals who have had surgery or transvestites who identify as female but have not had surgery find themselves struggling for acceptance by genuine women and denied the Affirmative Action which women won decades ago as women. The big fight today is transsexuals demanding equal participation in anti-patriarchy, pro-feminist parades and protests only to be told *NO* because 'you are not real women'. Transsexuals angrily respond by labeling feminists who oppose them as TERFs or Trans-Exclusionary Radical Feminists. SJWs love vague, nonsensical labels like TERF, cis-gender, red-baiting, and anti-Semitic. A TERF is a Feminist who resents men crashing their party by pretending to be women, exactly parallel to Blacks who resent whites crashing their party by pretending to be Black, or Jews who resent Gentiles trying to enter Israel claiming to be Jews. Feminists look with outrage on young men with estrogen treatments qualifying for Women's Title IX sports competitions beating the bejeezus out of young women because they continue to have male muscles and male height and male weight and male aggressiveness. In the end it seems that race and sex are more than just 'social constructs' after all, and not something that society – 'patriarchal' or otherwise – can simply choose.

These realities impede relations not only between Jews and Blacks, and between women and gays, but between women and Blacks. SJWs are mostly white women; but the goal of the Cult is to promote the interests of non-whites *at the expense of whites*. This creates unavoidable tension between white SJW women and SJWs 'of color'. But it's only temporary, since just as white male SJWs are expected to sacrifice themselves on the altar of a deceptive 'Equality', white males having been relegated to the legal status of a caste of Untouchables as the true goal of 'Inclusion', white female SJWs will also ultimately be expected to sacrifice themselves on the altar of a deceptive 'Diversity', as its opposite is finally implemented – a uniformity that excludes whites, which is the Cult's true goal.

In the end, as both Hillary and O.J. Simpson found in opposite ways, *race trumps gender*. This means that white female SJWs will eventually be forced to follow their rejected, self-hating Beta male white brethren into the dustbin of history, no apology for 'Whiteness' ever being enough to appease non-whites, apologies only exposing the victim as defenseless. White females, like it or not, will have to join the caste of white male Untouchables to live out their non-reproductive, carbon-free lives in tent cities on the crime-ridden streets of PC utopias like 'Woke' Seattle, San Francisco, Portland, and L.A. They may end up living in shantytowns asking for handouts from rich blacks, but at least they won't be 'racists'.

Blacks always put solidarity with Blacks over solidarity with whites. Witness how Blacks froze out Bernie and his white college kid Bros in favor of Biden who, though demented, grinningly celebrated the imminent racial extinction of whites on national TV.

Similarly, SJW women always put solidarity with women before solidarity with men. Male SJWs tend to be either under 25 years of age or over 65, based on whether their mental conditioning was recently acquired from Mass Media and College (not that there is any longer a difference) or was acquired in the days of Kennedy and Eisenhower, which means so far out of touch with today's America as to be fossilized.

Female SJWs can be any age at all. Despite all the high-falutin' talk about social constructs and evil patriarchy and their primitive eye-for-an-eye notion of pay-back reparations to achieve an illusory equality, when it comes to white society the PC Cult remains a predominantly Feminist enterprise and SJWs a mostly white female college phenomenon. Among SJWs, not only is masculinity not welcome – it is attacked as a display of patriarchy, spat upon, and condemned as the source of all evil. Only Beta Males who keep their privileged mouths shut are tolerated within the SJW Feminist fold.

Matriarchal SJWs have a 'school-marm stare' that one can scarce avoid where they frequent: a dull-as-dishwater frown of disapproval that drips condemnation and is directed at any man who dares show a masculine trait. In other words, any man who is too much like a man. Like Feminists, SJWs want their privileges and their equality too. When women stay at home and raise kids, letting their husbands work, that's okay with SJWs so long as she is free to abort, divorce, and obtain her Affirmative Action, likely keeping the house, the kids, and the car while doing so, and divorce courts run by SJW judges are quick to oblige them with outsized awards to the divorced ex-wife.

But when a man, for whatever reason, attempts to do the same and tries on the role of house-husband – SJWs feel threatened and emotionally revert to women's traditional role and attack him as a bum without a job. And the divorce courts are again quick to oblige, using the doctrine of 'imputed income', which is when the courts 'impute' an income to the man if he has no income due to unemployment or due to his having once accepted the role of house-husband.

Because, after all, everyone knows that even bad mothers are 'good enough' to keep their children in the event of a divorce compared to biologically deficient, xy-chromosomed men. And if a man does take time off to care for his kids, unlike women, he cannot put it on his resume or he will never be hired by employers again – especially by SJW Feminist employers. So here too it seems SJWs reject the notion of a 'social construct', falling back on biology when convenient.

This hypocrisy is another insight into the mental universe of SJWs: demanding that both sexes be treated equally when it benefits women, but when equality might infringe on one of their traditional rights as women and homemakers, loudly condemning equality. And, despite the trendy class-war rhetoric of Ivy League SJWs, there is no recognition of the dilemma, even plight, of lower-class women who lack the IQ to attend college, having been rejected by the same SJW college recruiters who proclaim that IQ is illusory, and who are faced with the choice of becoming either the house-wife of an auto mechanic, or – falling for the siren-song of privileged, upper-class Feminists by aborting, divorcing, and getting a job – ending up working at McDonald's for minimum wage for the rest of her life while shelving her kids in an expensive daycare.

For every 'liberated' upper class SJW woman teaching fake divinity-like Ethnic Studies courses on the public payroll, there are several lower-class women whose conversion to the Cult destroyed their happiness. The political power and economic gains that Ivy League SJWs enjoy have come *largely at the expense of unintelligent women* who were pushed to divorce their lower-class husbands and ended up single mothers flipping burgers next to horny Ali and racist Tyrone while their children rotted their lives away in daycares, having lost *both* parents.

Such children 'graduate' to drugs, depression, and suicide, after the child-support-paying father got tired of sleeping in his pickup truck and moved to Montana to start over. Like America's crime-ridden streets plagued by roving BLM gangs and MS-13, the collapse of the lower-class family too is part of the SJW Utopia pushed by America's privileged elites who persist in ignoring the realities of gender, race, and intelligence.

A working-class man with an IQ of 70, having once found a career he can handle, if he turns fifty and then loses his job to an immigrant, *cannot* be retrained for anything else useful to society. He does not have the intelligence to start over. A working-class woman with an IQ of 70, who we know will never complete college if she ever starts, has little chance of a happy and productive life apart from being the domestic partner in a long-term marriage to a man of similar background and similar IQ.

But SJWs never think about the plight of true working-class people like these, whose security and happiness are being destroyed by SJWs and their PC Cult in droves. The Cult's propaganda that women don't need husbands and that children don't need fathers is not only profoundly destructive to lower class women but has inflicted enormous damage on society, the divorce epidemic sending the crime rate soaring, triggering an explosion of domestic violence and gun sprees, and expanding medical costs and prisons by fueling an enormous drug epidemic by the children of broken families seeking substitutes for the family security they never had, which Cultists sweep under a rug by blaming the Second Amendment.

There are other genuine differences between the sexes. Men do not need safe spaces on a college campus. Men thrive in an open combative intellectual academic atmosphere where eccentricity pays, as Edward Dutton describes. They happily pursue fame and ego. But women desire consensus where eccentrics are pilloried and expelled, whatever they may have to contribute, because novelty makes women frightened and emotionally insecure and disrupts the female emotional need for superficial consensus-building, so women obsessively retreat to safe spaces to reproduce the family hearth, then try to make the entire college a safe space, then the country, and finally the world – a never-ending series of quixotic, impossible demands.

Women are rarely motivated by cutting-edge research, fame, new discoveries, or ego. They prefer to surround themselves with emotionally supportive female colleagues and diverse but submissive 'vibrant' immigrants to increase the women's pool for mate selection in finding a high-status man who will make them finally feel completely safe wherever she ventures and acquiring a prized mate with superior status.

This is why wherever women achieve significant numbers they immediately push for dropping barriers to entry so they can select from a global smorgasbord of men who are already wealthier and more powerful than they. A difficult task, given that female SJWs are themselves part of America's wealthy and powerful elite, and the 'vibrant immigrants' are a source of the uptick in campus rapes. Only ever greater numbers of immigrants can satisfy these contradictory and infinite demands.

Men desire high entry standards and national borders to curtail male competition, sympathy playing no part. Women seek to drop entry standards, even college SAT, and eliminate borders – allegedly 'for the children', but actually for the selfish needs of SJW women – in order to expand their mate selection choices and gratify their pathological altruism. To mix men and women professors in the same college department multiplies the confusion and inefficiency because their motives for why they teach and why they study and to what extent they may welcome immigrants are rarely the same.

When women attain control over the department or the college, the mission of the college fundamentally transforms from an entity that innovates and takes risks and toughens students, into an entity that conforms and protects and ceases to challenge, creating cohorts of sensitive, infantilized and infantilizing SJWs hiding in home-like safe spaces while keeping one eye open for powerful rich immigrant males, instead of creating tough adult men and sensible women primarily devoted to learning. Given Freud's opposition to mixing male and female students in the same classrooms, I think he would agree that the American concept of coeducation is deeply flawed and has seriously eroded the once eminent position of American education.

These conflicts reflect the dilemma of American society as a whole. Since modern philosophy, and the PC Cult in particular, are so heavily influenced by Nietzsche, this has left us with marvelous techniques for destroying society's values, but completely devoid of techniques for finding new ones. So today's colleges, arm-in-arm with the Mass Media, are adept at destroying values and undermining confidence and helping to plunge society into crime and anarchy, but have no way of constructing new values and restoring confidence in those institutions that every society needs in order to keep people alive.

The golem of the PC Cult has moved into this void and seeks to be that new religion which Nietzsche predicted must come. But in reality the PC Cult is nothing more than a false religion against life itself, a Death Cult of limitless guilt tripping and imputed sin: Nietzsche's Last Men – and Last Women – of Decadence.

VIRTUE-SIGNALING & WHITE KNIGHTS

If the Cult frame of mind is psychological but affects behavior like a virus, how is it spread? What makes the Cult's values so contagious? Where does it get its self-defense mechanism? How does the PC virus inoculate SJWs against 'contaminating' ideas that might cause an SJW to decide to reject the PC virus? The answers are (1) constant repetition, and (2) peer pressure via an in-built element of unconsciously but publicly signaling one's adherence to the Cult's values, which is called virtue-signaling. Like the Wuhan Coronavirus, the Cult's values spread from person to person long before any symptoms are visible. This happens by close association with people who already hold Cultic moral values or by participation in Cult-dominated organizations.

The groundwork is laid by constant media repetition from the Mass Media. This implants the basic values in a gradual process of psychological conditioning that changes the structure of the brain by unconsciously molding habits of thought into new patterns, bypassing objective information and rational reflection. Once the brain has been restructured and Cultic thought patterns firmly established by constant exposure to media broadcasts and indoctrinating classrooms, particularly along the lines of thinking in terms of superficial labels instead of empirical facts and in terms of moral approval or disapproval of every natural phenomenon, collective behavior is then instilled by peer pressure. Teenagers who may have been raised with an entirely different moral orientation will suddenly identify with Cultic collective categories shaped to comply with the principles of Diversity and Intersectionality, and their peers will then enforce a new pattern of behavior that requires public demonstrations of in-group loyalty.

This process reveals itself through group-loyal behavior, such as public ostracism of non-believers whom the in-group brands as heretics ('No Trump, no KKK') or who are threatened with physical assault ('Punch a Nazi'), and through routine displays of loyalty to the Cult by repeating Cult slogans and catechisms at every social event ('Diversity is our strength', 'Hands Up, Don't Shoot', 'Black Lives Matter', 'Our Mission is to Save the Planet'). This virtue-signaling serves the purpose of policing weaker group members, cautioning them that they too can be ostracized, and – like yellow and black colors on a hornet – warns outsiders that the SJW has been inoculated and her (or his) brain patterns altered so that rational discussion is no longer possible, only expressions of violence and hate. The entire process is unconscious and was described in the 1920s by Sigmund Freud's nephew, the Jewish psychologist Edward Bernays, the founder of modern public relations and theory of propaganda.

By such techniques, SJWs can be persuaded that Communists did *not* kill tens of millions of people but that Nazis *did* kill six million Jews, when evidence for the former is stronger than evidence for the latter. Or that Diversity is a strength when all evidence says it is a social weakness. Or that most mass shooters are white, when in fact most mass shooters are black, but under-reported. Or that blacks are victims of disproportionate police violence, when in fact more whites than blacks are victims of police violence, and white civilians are victims of black violence to a far greater extent than the reverse.

Or that courts fill prisons with kids who are caught with minor amounts of marijuana, when in fact courts convict mostly drug dealers caught with substantial amounts of narcotics or who have a record of other serious offenses. Or that all people everywhere are the same, when there is a profusion of thoroughly documented biological differences, including substantial differences in intelligence and behavioral predispositions, which point to the existence of fairly distinct races.

Or that men and women possess the same blank slate psychologically, when in fact men's psychology differs radically from women's psychology and that, statistically speaking, women are far more emotional and far more interested in relationships and children and romantic stories and 'saving refugees', while men are more interested in borders, territory, joining male-only physically active organizations, and engineering mechanisms of nature, and that these differences are rooted in biology, not environment, and cannot be easily changed. The number of men, for example, who would rather attend a recipe-sharing, quilt-sewing, coffee-klatch rather than work on a car, build a patio, or go shooting is minuscule, while most women will prefer the coffee-klatch.

These differences find ways to express themselves even among SJWs. Just as female SJWs often feel compelled to reclaim their traditional role of being the primary caretaker of children when men threaten to usurp this role, the marginal status of white males within the Cult leads them to proclaim their loyalty to the Cult more loudly and more often than do white females, frequently rushing to the 'defense' of female SJWs when the men perceive that the females may be in danger or their reputation traduced. These 'White Knights' thus gain sympathy and support from the socially superior females within the SJW group and avoid the necessity of gaining the females' favorable attention by getting themselves arrested for assaulting Proud Boys or shooting a Congressman.

Although the White Knight phenomenon, which is clearly contradictory to the PC Cult's stated values, is typically a variety of virtue-signaling, it can also happen at earlier stages, betraying an incomplete conversion of the White Knight to the Cult, his brain patterns not yet fully restructured. Thus, a White Knight SJW who holds open a door for a female SJW out of politeness may find himself insulted and cast into the bottom-most ranks of the SJW group as insufficiently 'woke', with no way left for him to regain status among other SJWs except to risk becoming a convicted felon by 'punching a Nazi' in view of the socially superior SJW women in order to regain his former status in the Cult.

11
SOCIALISM AND COMMUNISM

Nietzsche suggested that a fundamental instinct exists which he called the Will To Power (WTP). Since Nietzsche believed that will as a conscious autonomous mental process does not exist, all human activity being ultimately expressions of unpredictable physiological processes and unconscious motives, it is a poor choice of words. Rather Nietzsche's Will To Power is an extension of the Survival Instinct, an instinct that all living forms possess, surviving through domination of rivals and control of resources. While Nietzsche scornfully rejected individualistic Darwinism as an expression of 'English blockheads', his view of the WTP is Darwinian evolution extended to mass psychology, which he re-cast as various groups struggling for superior position within a single species, as opposed to inter-species competition or individual competition.

This is, of course, exactly the type of sociological and scientific research that has been prohibited in the U.S. ever since Boas and his Cultural Anthropology achieved hegemony in the 1930s. Today no group in the U.S. can be studied as a group *per se* but only as individuals – unless, of course, one is condemning whites or championing non-whites. This dominance is so complete that studying group evolutionary strategy is not merely disfavored in academia, it is prohibited throughout academia and, due to a series of Supreme Court rulings, it is illegal to implement any social policy based on such research – unless, of course, one is discriminating against white males, who are today's vilified Untouchables. Thus Arthur Jensen, Edward O. Wilson, Kevin MacDonald, J. Philippe Rushton, Richard Lynn, Charles Murray, James Watson, Edward Dutton and many other group evolutionary strategists, sociobiologists, and race realist scholars have been persecuted or banished from academia for 'wrong-think' in the past few decades for daring to investigate this taboo subject.

MacDonald's landmark studies of Jewish evolutionary strategy, in particular, are a direct outgrowth of Nietzsche's speculations of the WTP, though Nietzsche himself had no interest in identifying any particular ethnic group as a primary vehicle of Decadence. Nietzsche several times in his various works defended European Jews and condemned expressions of anti-Semitism and German nationalism, preferring wider European political movements.

However, in other passages, Nietzsche made it clear that he did hold Jews responsible for the 'slave morality' which he saw as the essence of Decadent Christianity and he believed that Jews of the 19th century were hardly distinguishable from the Jews of antiquity whom he blamed for inventing slave morality. In his view, expressed in several of his works and summed up in *Twilight of the Idols*, Christianity is effeminate and unnatural, seeking to control society through guilt, the preeminent weapon of inferior but resentful slaves, and he believed that Christians learned this deplorable technique from Jews.

Using the advantages which the more numerous class of slave-like 'Chandala' (Nietzsche's word for the caste of Untouchables in caste-ridden India) has over their natural rulers, the hereditary aristocracies, Christian priests in ancient times absorbed slave morality from the Jews and used it to achieve ideological hegemony over the late Romans. In more recent times, the aristocracy, or 'blond beasts', despite their apparent dominance, were in actuality fragile and they succumbed to the moral outlook of this corrupt priesthood (think of Holy Roman Emperor Henry IV on his knees to the Pope at Canossa, desperate to relieve his guilt), even if the aristocracy still had not yet lost all political power by Nietzsche's time in the late 19th century.

But by then a new force had appeared – democracy. Claiming to be secular, 19th century revolutionary democrats together with the more militant Marxian Socialists attacked what remained of the beaten-down aristocracy using the same slave morality that Christian priests had used for centuries, and with even greater success than had the Catholic Church. Recruiting all the strands of modern scientism and sociology, Marxian Socialism, especially, challenged traditional privileges across Europe.

Socialism was not as new and innovative, however, as Socialists liked to believe. Marxian Socialism, as the only political socialism, was hardly distinguishable from a Protestant Millerite tent revival once one put aside the revolutionary rhetoric: Socialists believed in an imminent Heaven on Earth, which was the triumph of Socialism after the Revolution; in Original Sin, which was the traditional Christian sin of greed (when have Jews ever condemned greed in their business dealings with Gentiles?); in a Satan, which was the Russian Tsar; and in a Sacrificed God who promised to return to Earth in the End Times to rule Earth forever, which became the Proletariat, the new industrial workers. It was their blood, spilled in union protests and laboring in dark, dangerous Satanic mills that earned by their sacrifice the coming Heaven of Marxist Socialism and which would redeem humanity. All this, the new prophet Karl Marx, the St. Paul of Socialism, promised in Das Kapital, his holy text which 'revealed' the inexorable Laws of History and the imminent doom of the exploiters.

Strangely, though, Socialism never took hold among the working classes of Europe, neither among the industrial proletariat nor among workers in more traditional occupations. One of the issues was that the leading intellectuals of Socialism were Jews. Marx was the son of a converted Jewish rabbi from a long line of Jewish rabbis, and everywhere international Socialists congregated, Jews dominated.

Another issue was that European Jews were urban. They did not farm. There was no Jewish peasantry anywhere in Europe so there was no connection between urban Jews who were naturally attracted to the idea of an urban industrial proletariat and Christian peasants who saw nothing in Marx's urbanized Socialism that might benefit them. The absence of Jews from field labor was so complete that the Russian word for peasant even today is *krestyan*, or 'Christian'.

In the cities, one of the largest cohorts of skilled workers was furniture artisans. By the 1880s, this traditional profession was collapsing and artisans widely unemployed; their main experience with Jews was door-to-door Jewish salesmen selling factory-made furniture produced in new urban factories owned by Jews – the very factories that were driving the Christian artisans out of business. Just as Jewish-owned Google and Home Depot are driving small Gentile enterprises in droves out of business today. So Christian artisans resented Jews and rejected Jewish Socialism. Finally, by 1890 it became obvious that Marxism as a politicized workers' movement had failed because the working classes as a whole had succeeded in negotiating higher wages and social benefits which made armed Revolution unnecessary.

But then came Communism. In the 1890s, realizing that the time for a mass spontaneous workers' revolution had gone, Lenin and the exiled community of Russian Marxists embraced a new idea. They would henceforth devote themselves to overthrowing 'bourgeois' governments by means of an international conspiracy of armed professional revolutionaries, without regard for legal or democratic formalities, boycotting elections and refusing to serve in parliaments even if offered, as the Socialist 'opportunists' of the Second International had mistakenly done. Without the support of 'the masses', whose interests they purported to serve but who never backed them, the goal of Lenin's Bolsheviks was the armed seizure of power followed by comprehensive nationalization of industry, land, and media, which they never doubted would finally usher in the elusive Workers' Paradise that Marx had predicted.

Communism, however, was at least as dominated by Jews as had been Marxist Socialism – in fact, was even more Jewish. While Socialism was a Jewish-led movement of former Christians who perceived themselves to be secularized champions of 'human rights' but still clung to many Christian concepts and values, Communism on the other hand was *majority Jewish*. At least 80%

of the Bolshevik leaders from the Communist Party's Central Committee up to the Politburo were ethnic Jews born and raised in Tsarist Poland, or who had taken up residence in Russia's largest cities after the Tsars ceased enforcing the Pale of Settlement, or Jews in the Ukraine where the Tsars, at great expense, attempted to resettle with generous subsidies many of their burgeoning Jewish population in the late 19th century.

The Bolsheviks' security organizations, in particular, were run by ethnic Jews. The Communist Party's Gulag concentration-camp administrators and personnel and the brutal Cheka (later NKVD, later KGB) were mostly staffed by ethnic Jews. Like many Jews today, these are not always easy to identify by historians because many had changed their names under the Tsars under pressure to assimilate, or their fathers had changed their names and the sons kept their father's Christianized name, though remaining Jewish in sympathy, in associations, and in self-identification.

The first head of the Cheka, Dzerzhinsky, is often given as an example of a non-Jew in an effort to prove that Bolsheviks were not Jews and that Russian Communism was not a Jewish phenomenon. However, although Dzerzhinsky is a Polish name which he acquired from his father who was a 'minor noble', it remains likely that Dzerzhinsky's father was a Jewish convert as he was raised in a town in east Poland that was dense with Jews and he owned no land, which was a requirement for Polish nobility, and there is no trace of this title of nobility preceding him, so it seems likely that Dzerzhinsky's father was a Jew who had been awarded the title as an honorary for some service.

And although one of the first acts of the Bolsheviks after they seized power in October 1917 was to outlaw all expressions of anti-Semitism, no other ethnic group or religion received similar protections. While synagogues were protected by the Bolsheviks and Jewish rabbis were recruited into the state en masse due to the Bolsheviks' need for literate cadres – Jewish rabbis being among the most literate people in Russia and more literate on average than Orthodox priests – Christianity, on the other hand, was outlawed and many churches were demolished and many Orthodox priests shot outright by the new Jewish-run Cheka, all on direct orders from the 'non-Jew' Lenin.

It would still be unjustified, however, to label Communism as simply a 'Jewish movement'. Although Jews prospered in the early days of Bolshevism to the point that non-Jews began to see them as especially privileged within the Party, Jews among the Bolshevik leadership were largely annihilated in Stalin's purges in the late 1930s. The only Jew on the Politburo to survive into old age, of which this writer is aware, was Lazar Kaganovitch, the architect of the Ukrainian famine. (He survived perhaps because his sister was allegedly intimately involved with Stalin.) In fact, the distinction between Jewish Communists and non-Jewish Communists remained notable throughout the interwar period, i.e., between World Wars I & II with the Jewish Communists enjoying more benefits than non-Jewish Communists.

Stalin prevailed over Trotsky in the 1920s precisely because Trotsky was Jewish while Stalin was not, and Stalin had studied for a time in a Christian seminary as proof of his non-Jewish background. Communists do not like to admit this. Stalin also openly criticized 'rootless cosmopolitans' – everyone knew this was code for Jews. As late as 1939, even though Stalin had married two Jewish women, he substituted the non-Jew Molotov ('the Hammer') for the Jew Litvinov, as his chief negotiator with Hitler.

Even though Bolshevik Communism was more Jewish than Marxian Socialism had been, Russian Communism still showed many of the same Christian features that Marxism had shown. Communism had a Pope in his Vatican, which was Stalin in the Kremlin who provided the last word on Communist theology. It had a hierarchically organized priesthood, who were Russian members of the Communist Party, many though not all of Jewish background. It had an international network of sympathizers, who were those Ashkenazi Jews who had migrated to Europe and the U.S., many becoming esteemed academics or rising to occupy high political positions and some even working inside the spy agencies of Western countries like Britain and the U.S.

The loyalty of these 'fifth-column' Jews to Moscow – and their disloyalty to their host nations – could be absolutely relied upon by Stalin, their greatest 'success' being the transfer of knowledge of the Atom Bomb from Los Alamos to the Soviet Union in the late 1940s, enabling Stalin to explode his first atomic bomb in 1949. For this espionage the Communist Jewish couple, the Rosenbergs, were executed in the U.S. in 1950 despite huge demonstrations in New York City of Jews sympathetic to the Soviet Union asserting the Rosenbergs' innocence.

Communism had a powerful Marketing Machine – the network of newspapers and media and movie production companies owned by Jews in Europe and the U.S., and everywhere else in the Anglosphere, all of which ferociously defended the Rosenbergs as innocent victims of what was soon labeled 'McCarthyism'.

Communism had a series of 'churches' – Jewish reform synagogues in the West, radiating from New York City, which was the center of support for Communism in America. It had a Second Coming of Christ, the imminent Christian Heaven on Earth, which was the Communist Utopia, indeed which had ostensibly already arrived in the form of Stalin's Soviet Union which was systematically portrayed as the Workers' Paradise in Jewish-staffed organs like *The New York Times*, and in many Hollywood movies.

It had Original Sin, which was the greed of the capitalist world as evident in their exploitation of private employment. It had a Satan, who was at first Trotsky, then Hitler, then every American President (Satan is important in Christianity – not important at all in Judaism). It even had an army of Crusaders sworn to spread the Communist Faith globally by military means, which was Stalin's Red Army, and which provided military training in Moscow and plentiful arms transfers to any revolutionary group that promised to challenge 'capitalist' powers anywhere in the world so long as they maintained an unquestioning allegiance to the Russian Communist Party and to Stalin.

True, Communists expressed extreme hatred for their enemies and had no tolerance for Christian love, charity, or forgiveness – and 'sacred hate' against Gentiles is as integral to Judaism as 'sacred rage' against infidels is integral to Islam. But aside from that, the only significant difference between Marxian Socialism and Leninist Communism, apart from Lenin abandoning all pretense to democracy, was that in place of Russia's missing proletariat, Jews seemed to be substituting themselves. Stalin ended that with his bloody purges, which, directly or indirectly, killed millions. It is possible that Jewish doctors had their revenge on Stalin in 1953 when he died of medical neglect just as he seemed about to unleash a second, more complete purge of Jews from the Communist Party in Russia.

There was never a purge of Jews from Communist parties outside the Soviet Union, however, and most Jews in the West denied that any purge had ever taken place in Russia. Tired of waiting like Godot for their Messiah – after all, two thousand years is a long time to wait for anyone – some European Jews had long entertained the notion that Jews could be their own Messiah, that Jews as a group were foreordained to lead the world to paradise under the doctrine of *Tikkun Olam* ('repairing the world'), and that this was the true meaning of being Yahweh's Chosen People.

For some, this notion had its expression as Jews substituting themselves for the long-absent proletariat in the Soviet Union. With Stalin's heel-turn against them in Russia, this variant lost popularity. Jews in the West, however, had already begun to abandon the 'anti-Semitic' Messiah Stalin and embrace the more internationalist Trotsky, who was after all a true Jew, and when all Communist sects finally faded from the scene in the 1960s, the idea of Tikkun Olam enjoyed a revival among supposedly 'secular' Jews.

1 2
WHERE HAVE ALL THE CHRISTIANS GONE?

As described above, the PC Cult is not synonymous with Jews. The doctrine of Tikkun Olam is also not synonymous with Political Correctness, and that is not where this analysis is headed. Although Jews, especially Jewish professors, are indeed the priesthood of the PC Cult, just as Jews were the brutal 'Jesuit' commissars of 20th century Soviet Communism, and Jews were the intellectual leaders of 19th century Marxian Socialism, the PC Cult remains predominantly – one might almost say again and still – primarily Christian in its values and inspiration.

Where Christ died for Mankind's sins, the Cult sees Mother Earth, the ultimate 'person of color', dying for the sins of Men: greed and racism. Greed and hate are sins to Christians, not to Jews, who often regard them on the contrary as virtues when directed against Gentiles. Effeminacy is also not a Jewish trait even though Jewishness is traced through the mother, but specifically Christian. Catholic priests regarded supernal masculinity as qualitatively superior to earthly femininity, having inherited this notion from the ancient Greeks of the corrupt Hellenistic period, and thus condoned male homosexuality as spiritually superior to marriage and children, even holding out effeminate males and castrati as moral ideals – SJWs have merely flipped this and regard earthly femininity and castrated males as spiritually superior to earth-dominating, virile heterosexual men. In the PC Cult there remains a God (now a Goddess) who died, or is dying, for our sins – this is a very Christian concept, and very distant from Tikkun Olam, Jews having no intention of dying for anyone, not even in the course of world-repairing social work.

It is no accident that SJWs call the living Earth Mother 'Gaia' or 'Gaea', similar to Gay-ness, just as it is no accident that Amazon is the most successful online business. 'Amazons' were the armed female warriors of ancient times who did not tolerate men. Both names point to Environmentalism and worship of a powerful female Nature as modern versions of ancient Earth Mother worship. Both names, as manifestations of the PC Cult, attract wealthy influential Feminists.

Voluntary emasculation and worship of effeminacy have always been an integral part of religious cults that worship Earth Mothers. The ancient Cult of Cybele in Asia Minor, where the Amazons of legend supposedly lived, encouraged male followers to emasculate themselves with a knife, and many did. Catholicism for centuries tolerated gay priests who organized the castration of boys for choirs and presumably sexual services. The Heaven's Gate suicide cult which was begun by Unitarians and was a branch of the PC Cult, encouraged castration of its male members, performed on many by surgeons in Mexico. Today's PC Cult, with its worship of gayness and hyper-condemnation of masculinity, is more subtle but no different. It too encourages its male followers to emasculate themselves to atone for their sins against the Goddess, the Great Earth Mother. Like male followers of Cybele, many are happy to do so, and like Jonestown many endorse mass suicide.

All religions have a 'Golden Age'. This is a mythical time when the religion was born, when its values took effect and became real, the time of its Creation, marked by the death of its eponymous sacrificial Founder / Hero who died in the act of Creation and whose perfection the faithful are supposed to emulate. The PC Cult has this too. It commemorates the Golden Age when the modern PC Cult was created in its present form: celebrating civil rights marches, worshipping saints such as Rosa Parks, Emmet Till, MLK, and every Black and a few Jews who died in the fight to desegregate the South near the sacred shrine of Selma, Alabama.

All cults commemorate the time of Creation with periodic festivals and solemn rituals and special music that serve to remind the Cultists of their Golden Age and the holy sacrifice of their Founders. These festivals reenact the Creation, projecting the faithful back into the time of sacred myth, historical facts being irrelevant to that myth; indeed it is sacrilegious to SJWs even to suggest that facts might be relevant.

The special music is songs by Bob Dylan, Pete Seeger, "Southern Man" by Crosby, Stills, Nash & Young, updated by contemporary 'hymns' of Cultic 'sacred hate' by PC Cult bands like Rage Against the Machine, and old black church hymns such as "We Shall Overcome", and perhaps newer ones yet to reach this writer's ears. The PC Cult has many festivals and many rituals – these reenact the events of the Golden Age of Heroism when the Founders achieved Salvation by vanquishing Evil Whiteness at Selma and creating the Properly Ordered Matriarchal Universe out of the Chaos of Patriarchal Whiteness. Black History Month is the most widespread festival, but the sacred 'coalition' protest march against everything white and male is the preeminent ritual, now with an obligatory blocking of profane street traffic.

While Black History Month is the most widespread Cultic festival for blacks, constantly reinforcing the notion that melanin is uniquely sacred to the Earth Mother, for white SJWs the primary festival is rather Burning Man. That a 'Man' is burned at Burning Man again is no accident. The Cult offers 'Man' – symbolizing all men – as sacrifices to Mother Earth, the effigy fixed to the Earth via a sacred pyramid of wood. Pyramids are by nature Earth markers, particularly if they have a hollow, chthonic, egg-like interior. By burning men in effigy, the Burning Man festival seeks not only to reinforce the social superiority of female SJWs over male SJWs, reminding them of their status as only one step above the outcast Untouchables, but to cast a spell over Nature, to control it and place the Earth Goddess in the service of Cultish SJWs, just as when incense was burned at the feet of the Greek Goddess Athena or the Phrygian Goddess Cybele when believers voiced their appeals to the goddesses. The sacrifice nourishes Gaia while it promotes Matriarchy and emasculated Gayness, and a carbon-footprint-free Sacred Earth.

It is also not an accident that the Burning Man ritual occurs in an Earth-centered pyramid of dead wood rather than in a living tree, since living trees are sacred to Earth-centered Environmentalism and therefore cannot be burned, as opposed to Druids who burned living trees along with human sacrifices, or the human sacrifices that were hanged in trees like the Irminsul which were trees sacred to Odin, a Nordic male sky god, a 'Nazi' god in the theocratic language of the PC Cult. In today's Cult, living people can be burned, but not living trees. Burning Man takes place yearly in a desert, deliberately far from any location where its rituals might harm living vegetation belonging to the Sacred Earth Mother, excepting that which is incidental to an almost empty desert.

Climate change is core to the PC Cult because it is the ultimate expression of valuing the passive Earth Mother over evil masculine dominating activities. These activities manifest themselves as 'Whiteness'. Among Cultists, melanin, like pyramids, is an Earth-sign. The darker the worshipper, the closer to the Earth Mother is his or her 'essence' (not 'soul' because 'scientific' cultists believe in New Age 'spiritual essences', not in religious souls). The holy substance of melanin – the special mark of the Earth Mother's special People of Color – preserves them from sin, which substitutes for the Christian God's grace. The phrase Black Lives Matter is another religious catechism because it proclaims this special quality attaching to melanin. 'Only Black Essences are Holy' would be a more direct formulation.

Tenured professor Leonard Jeffries, Jr., former department chair of Black Studies at the City College of New York, of the City University of New York (CUNY) states this clearly. According to Jeffries, whites are "ice people" devoid of empathy and kindness while Africans are "sun people" who are compassionate and peaceful, their melanin enabling them to "negotiate the vibrations of the universe" which makes them inherently superior to whites. Thus people with melanin can do no wrong; their melanin sacralizes their every act, rendering them blameless and free of liability – a society of racial Brahmins who, by the will of the Earth Mother, are not or should not be required to labor but are entitled to survive on tribute ('reparations') from the lower castes in exchange for their sacrifices before and during the Golden Age and for their on-going suffering ('exhaustion from being Black') as they struggle for spirituality on behalf of the Earth Goddess, who, since melanin is the primary marker of sacredness, is necessarily rooted in Africa and whose preeminent signs are everything African.

For SJWs, Africa is the ultimate Safe Space because a Safe Space is ultimately not about protection from violence, but protection from Whiteness. That's the whole point of Safe Spaces, which are more properly termed Sacred Spaces, the SJWs' 'mosques' where the Chaos of Whiteness is not allowed. If a trip to Africa is not yet as obligatory for SJWs as a Muslim's trip to Mecca, SJWs may seek to vacation from the 'exhausting' presence of white males and seek 'safety' from their contaminating Whiteness by going to Costa Rica or Jamaica, or any other country closer to the equator that is darker than white America and has better facilities than distant and backward Africa.

Haiti, therefore, may not qualify because, although the darkest of countries in the Western Hemisphere, it has even fewer modern facilities than most of Africa. If a trip to any place outside the U.S. is impractical, then a retreat to the nearest Shrine of the Black Madonna, often located on a city's Martin Luther King Boulevard, will do. There one can gaze upon images of the PC Cult's Africanized Great Earth Mother.

Just as caste-ridden Hindus have degrees of 'enlightenment', the more melanin People of Color possess, the more enlightened and holier they are, and the more blessed and blameless and the more entitled they are to receiving reparations, not because their acts are 'innocent' in themselves but because the actors are blessed by their nature and can do no wrong even if they try, least of all by harming a member of the lowest cast of melanin-deficient Untouchables and are sent to prison as a result.

This is reflected in even more PC linguistic fakery: when Blacks commit crimes they are described as 'teens' or 'youths', implying they have no free will and cannot be held responsible, and their photos are often obscured by the Media – even if they are over twenty-one. But when whites commit crimes they are described as 'Nazis' or 'White Nationalists' the instant their race is identified and their pictures are always widely displayed and shared on Facebook in order to expose their insubordination and their disrespect for the melanin-endowed higher castes.

By definition, under the PC Cult, punishing sacred People of Color by sending them to prison is itself a crime against Nature, greater than any crime that the Person Of Color may have perpetrated against a white Untouchable. It is not necessary to be completely black to qualify for this immunity from law enforcement – even a small amount of melanin (for now at least) is sufficient to be judged 'enlightened' and thus entitled to government support and prompt release by various Innocence Projects from imprisonment by whites. The 'innocence' pertains not to their acts, but to their salvatory melanin.

But the melanin must be visible to other Blacks. A spray-on tan, or a 23AndMe report showing a Nigerian great-grandmother, won't suffice. This will certainly change as the Cult gains more power. Eventually only the blackest of Blacks will be accorded top honors and privileges as a 'one-drop of whiteness' rule pushes mulattos like Obama down the Intersectional ladder.

Again, the basic structure of this is inherited from Christianity, with a Black Earth Mother substituted for a pale male Christ-as-an-Annually-Resurrected-Vegetation-God, with melanin substituting for baptism and conferring perfect unconditional grace. This is not Socialism, Communism, Cultural Marxism, or Tikkun Olam. It is Christianity unleashed, Christianity collapsed into a Black Hole, its asymptote of altruism reaching infinity – the traditional traits of charity and turning the other cheek having burgeoned in the PC Cult into a limitless pathology, a mass psychosis driving its members to happily embrace Jonestown-like mass suicide, offering their empty melanin-absent lives as reparation for imagined racism and alleged greed-induced climate change at the feet of their new deity, the Universalist Politically Correct African Earth Mother – an Environmentalist Black Madonna, a female Allah of the Earth, a Westernized feminized Rasta god Jah.

Sometimes the urge to suicide among ex-Christians who have converted to the PC Cult is so great that even melanin won't stop them – witness the People's Temple of San Francisco, a Church of Diversity before it became the official state religion of America, which moved to Guyana under the leadership of the self-hating white pastor Jim Jones. Once there, almost their entire congregation of over 900 members, most of whom were sacred 'People of Color', committed suicide when a visit by a white Congressman persuaded Jones that armed attack by racist capitalist white America was imminent. Jones had his followers shoot the Congressman before ordering the rest to drink poisoned Kool-Aid, coining the phrase 'don't drink the Kool-Aid' as a metaphor for 'don't become so committed to a fanatical cause that you let your brain fall out'.

But letting their brains fall out is what SJWs do. Today's PC Cult is the People's Temple of Jim Jones writ large and enforced by law in every school and business in the nation as the new state religion by government-subsidized PC Diversity Commissars. Every Democrat running for office is another Jim Jones; every Democrat Party branch is another People's Temple. But these SJWs are not content to simply commit suicide – they are determined to take the rest of the world with them, preparing seas of poisoned Kool-Aid for a guest-list of billions. Just as weeds are more important to these SJWs than men, the Earth Mother's dirt is more important to them than the lives of billions of people. In this rush to global destruction, White Genocide is just the beginning of its lethal agenda as the Cult-inspired conflict in Ukraine threatens to trigger global nuclear war with Russia.

Amazon-Earth worship; white Christian guilt expressed by zero children; mental coma induced by tax-subsidized marijuana like 'soma' in the novel *Brave New World*; and repetitive 24/7 ever more superficial programming in Cult-run 5G global corporate networks run by Globo-Homo, family-hating, pedophile, childless gays; militant PC Vegans sabotaging farmers markets and steakhouses for sinning against the Earth Mother's sacred climate and Her sacred animals – which means any animal, even bacteria – while concocting vegetarian diets for their child-substituted, meat-starved cats and dogs; sacralization of melanin as intrinsic to the Earth; media encouragement of violent crimes against whites; suppression of free speech and majority voting as 'violent' expressions of sinful anti-environmental racism; scorn for private enterprise because it is individualistic and therefore sinful – unless of course the enterprise endorses suppressing the free speech of whites, or is used to promote the Unified Universalist theocratic platform. . . all of these are integral to SJWs and today's murderous PC Cult.

And just as Socialists hated the Tsar as their chosen Satan, and Communists hated Hitler as their chosen Satan, today's PC Cult SJWs hate white male Republican Presidents as their chosen Satan, not for what they do, but for who they are: non-apologetic white males who reject the status of Untouchable and who still believe in orderly democratic principles. First was Nixon, then Reagan, then the Bushes, then Trump. All of these were viciously attacked in their day as 'Satan' or 'literally Hitler' by globalist Leftists in the press, on TV, in endless ritualistic 'coalition' violent protest marches, and in the spiteful, mocking hate speech of endless queues of Jewish Hollywood comedians, happy to use their privileged pulpits and instant privileged access to global media to help the hated Gentiles destroy themselves.

And where Communist Parties had gangs of Red Guards to dominate the streets of Germany and Russia who attacked any public demonstration by nationalists, no matter how lawful or peaceful, today's PC Cult has Antifa units as its street militia, led by SJW professors and often flying the very same 'anti-Fascist' flags used by the Red Guards in the 1920s in Europe or in the

1960s in China, to attack anyone who points out that SJWs are a suicide cult, that they are hurrying to their own destruction like captains of doomed Titanics joyously steering at every iceberg while gustily singing "Onward PC Soldiers".

The Cult even has its own array of saints: as the Communist saints Marx, Lenin, and Trotsky fade into oblivion, joined by the Liberal saints FDR, JFK, and RFK, all too white to make PC Saint First-Class. . . new martyrs for the New Faith have taken their place: MLK, Mandela, Bishop Tutu, Obama, Trayvon Martin, Michael Brown, George Floyd. Selected for their melanin, these have been ascribed semi-miraculous qualities and reinvented as divine heroes who did no wrong. Indeed, Obama was awarded a Nobel Peace Prize merely for taking office, the SJW Swedes on the Nobel Committee not waiting for him to die before rushing to declare him a full-fledged Saint First-Class, virtue-signaled into snow-blindness by his dazzling melanin.

The 'Reverend Dr.' Martin Luther King, Jr., a militant Communist drug-fueled philanderer who plagiarized a divinity degree that any illiterate could have obtained with his eyes closed, has become indistinguishable from Gandhi – another PC saint who was anything but an advocate of peace as SJWs like to imagine. HRC and Bernie remain a step away from full sainthood only because they still live, but they may receive promotion to PC Saint Second-Class after death if it is sudden and mysterious and can be blamed on 'racists' and 'right-wingers', as their deaths will be whatever the truth, because they are 'down with the Cause' of the Black Earth Mother and Her Sacred Climate and because they worship Earth-melanin and because they routinely condemn whites who are tainted by the visible absence of the Earth Mother's sacred sign of Blackness.

Today's PC Cult is not organized in a top-down fashion as was the former global Communist Party, but the religious nature of the movement is even more pronounced than was Communism. One might say that where Communism paralleled 16th century Catholicism of the Counter-Reformation in its organization, centered in the Kremlin which served as its Vatican, today's PC religion is more similar to the disorganized but even more millenarian tent-revival Protestant movements of the 19th century.

Christians became the new Chosen People by excluding Jews. PC Cultists have become the new Chosen People by excluding whites – white being the color of ice and death as opposed to the red of life-blood and the fruit of African tropics. Christians are sanctified by baptism, a symbolic regeneration of the Cosmos on a personal individual level. Cultists are sanctified by melanin, an inborn sacred substance that releases all 'vibrants' from sin, guaranteeing them salvation, and substituting for Christian faith because melanin is the essence of the sacrificial Great Earth Mother. Melanin therefore is the literal blood of the new Christ, sanctifying a new Chosen People.

'Racism' sums this up as the ultimate sin because racism is seen by the Cult as the sin of disloyalty, of apostasy, a betrayal of the Mother Goddess, an attack on God Herself. If the Earth Mother's special 'people of color' are suffering in the Earth Mother's original homeland, Africa, it can only be due to climate change, which itself can only be due to evil spells cast by Satanic racists (Whites and Republicans), who, condemned by the Goddess in Her act of Universal Creation to forever lack Her sacred substance, and due to operation of the sacred principles of Social Constructs, Deconstruction, and Intersectionality are forever denied the holiness of insight that the 'exhausting' experience of 'systemic racism' and 'racial discrimination' bring to Her Chosen People of Color, who bear the burdensome but holy sign of melanin. Thus, the common proclamation that Whites cannot understand 'the Black experience' because – since they lack holy melanin – they necessarily lack the mystical insight that melanin bestows by its sacredness.

Like whites in South Africa, whites in the West have thus been permanently branded by the Cult with an unerasable Original Sin, making them permanent infidels and heretics, subject to attack by the righteous. The American South and South Africa were thus the Petri dishes, the rehearsals of what is now happening throughout the U.S. with our mushrooming black on white crime and its routine excusal by SJW judges, who refuse to impose bail or prosecute if the accused bears the sacred sign of melanin and if the accused blames his conduct on 'racism', the modern equivalent of voodoo or 'the devil made me do it.'

The sacralization of melanin has gone so far that mentally conditioned whites are adopting black culture to the exclusion of other cultures, even their own. The Hollywood media today claims that no other 'culture' exists except the culture of those blessed with the sacred marker of melanin – that whites indeed have no culture, whether in Sweden, Britain, or the U.S. This is just another way of saying that Chaos ('Whiteness') by definition can have no culture because Chaos by definition has no form, and can have no form, until its form is created and imposed by the Great Creator, the African Earth Mother.

Under the Bolsheviks in Russia, ethnic Russians were called 'white niggers' by Walter Duranty, the Communist-supporting, Pulitzer Prize-winning, *New York Times* reporter posted in Moscow who told the Times good things about Stalin and Communism because that was what the Jewish-run Times wanted to hear. The minority-worshipping Bolsheviks regarded white Russians as third-class citizens who were completely expendable, Moscow first taking their rights, then their religion, and finally taking their food and exporting it in exchange for military equipment to build up the Red Army into the largest army the world had seen, causing millions of 'white nigger' Ukrainians to starve to death in the Holodomor, implemented by Stalin's henchman **Lazar Kaganovich**, after their crops were stolen and exported.

Today in the U.S. we have 'wiggers', whites whose brains have been so conditioned by the Cult and its propaganda media that they have adopted the dress and language and mannerisms of uneducated ghetto blacks, thinking that this will keep them from being labeled white racist Untouchables. But, as described above, nothing can save whites from being branded as Untouchables because that depends on who they are, not on what they do or what they say. Under the PC Cult, White equals racist – period. And it is only a short step from having one's culture canceled, to having one's job, bank account, and finally one's life canceled. That is how SJWs roll. . .

Still, the PC Cult is not exactly Christianity turned upside down. There is another movement, a broader social movement, that is friendlier to Tikkun Olam, which is exerting a pull on the entire U.S. This is the strangest development of all – the disappearance of formal Christian sects across all denominations and from all political parties throughout the Western world, and their reappearance as. . . what?

Christianity, of course, began as a Jewish sect. It was only St. Paul, the ex-Jew, who abandoned the Jewish law and preached a Judaism without the Law to the Greek world – a corrupt world during the Hellenistic era that was awash in homosexuality and Earth Mother worship and military weakness, seeking refuge from Roman militarism in philosophy and Platonism.

As described above, Christianity absorbed the slave morality of the Jews, who never missed a chance to proclaim that the world belonged to the meek and the sinful, and that, as the most meek and the most sinful, the future therefore belonged to Jews alone. All Christians needed was the Greek philosophical idea of Logos married to the classical pagan cult of an annually dying and resurrected god of vegetation, and they founded a new imperial religion that succeeded in reviving the Roman Empire for another 1500 years while frustrated Jews looked on in surprise from impotent, bitter exile.

But what happens when Christ no longer commands the faithful? What happens when, as Nietzsche noted and deplored, God finally – irrevocably – dies? What do Christians do when Jesus is no longer on the cross, when his sacrifice is seen as pointless, when his resurrection is proven scientifically impossible, when the whole suffering, death, and resurrection becomes, in a word, blarney? What happens to what was once a minor Jewish cult separated from the bulk of Jewry by little more than faith in a dusty myth that no one – least of all, Christians – any longer accepts as true? The theologian Rudolf Bultmann recognized that without the myth of the Suffering God, the Crucifixion, and the Resurrection, Christianity ceases to exist. He correctly observed that without myth there can be no Christianity. And without Christianity, Christians have no cause, no goal, no longer any guide to life, no motivation even for self-defense.

Are there any true Christians left? What megachurch in the U.S. is willing to send soldiers to fight and die for the Cross, as it once sent Crusaders and Templars by the thousands into Spain, Malta, Sicily, and Palestine, or to conquer New Worlds for their faith? How many Baptist Churches today are willing to send armed volunteers to ports of entry, ready to lay down their lives to stop the on-going invasion of infidel immigrants? Not one.

Today's 'Christian' churches are too busy endorsing abortion, gay marriage, Diversity, Intersectionality, and providing Sanctuaries for virulently anti-Western and anti-Christian criminal illegals – while sending planeloads of pacifist volunteers to Africa to 'save' the Earth Mother's special People of Color – while doing nothing to save white South Africans from torture and genocide at the hands of those same People of Color. For centuries, 'White' was synonymous with European and Christian. Now both 'White' and Christian are synonymous with abortion, gayness, capitulation, and suicide.

Where have all the Christians gone? We know many have embraced the PC Cult. But not all. Among Evangelicals and those who still cling to 'their guns and Bibles', it's not Mother Earth that has replaced Christianity, and not Tikkun Olam – the idea that Jews have a special role to 'heal' the world through social justice as their own Messiah. No – it's the realization that, once faith in Jesus disappears, Christianity reverts to being a minor Jewish sect. This should not seem strange. Christianity and Judaism have always been blood brothers, always inseparable; Christian Big Brother has at times scolded his incorrigible Jewish Little Brother, but they are brothers nonetheless. Writer E. Michael Jones repeatedly asserts that Christians are forbidden by their faith from "harming the Jew", and Christian pastors repeatedly state that the New Testament 'fulfills' the Jewish Old Testament rather than negates it.

'We are all Jews now' is the clarion call of Republicans, summed up in the phrase 'Judeo-Christian tradition', even though it is more accurate to speak of a 'Judeo-Islamic tradition' versus a 'Greek-Christian tradition', as Republicans should know. There is nothing traditional about the so-called 'Judeo-Christian tradition'; it is a recent invention of faithless Christians who have nothing left to cling to after the death of their God but their ancient blood brothers: Jews and Judaism.

Modern 'Christianity', therefore, seems to be returning to the bedrock from whence it came – back to Judaism, symbolized by Israel. For Republicans, junkets to Tel Aviv have entirely replaced junkets to Lourdes or the Vatican or Constantinople or even to Moscow, one of the few remaining white and formally Christian nations on Earth. As Protestants embrace the principles of the PC Cult like Diversity and Zero Children and blaming whites and only whites for Climate Change, they find that they have replaced praising a defunct Christ with praising Jews and Judaism, represented by the modern State of Israel and Israel's religion of The Jewish Holocaust, as if praising Israel and building more and more Holocaust Museums will make up for the death of their Christian God.

This seems outlandish, even to this writer – except when one realizes that there has been a broad movement within Protestantism for centuries in the direction of Judaization of the various denominations, beginning with the Pilgrims and Anabaptists and East European Unitarians (the 'Joo-nitarians'). In effect, the more that Christians have lost their Christian faith over the years, the more Jewish they have become, almost without realizing it.

As Christianity loses its force, its followers are returning to their mother faith – many by way of the PC Cult as a sort of halfway house for ex-Christians who are not quite ready to don phylacteries and yarmulkes, but almost as many ex-Christians are taking the route of openly praising nationalistic Israelis and Israel as intrinsically more authentic than the U.S., burdened as the U.S. is with a dead Christianity. The collapse of Christianity is so complete that even Pope Francis spoke of Judaism as being more authentic than Catholicism: "Inside every Christian is a Jew." He has never said: "Inside every Jew is a Christian," as one might expect from the head of the world Catholic faith.

The odd result is that mind-numbed SJWs in the PC Cult seem at times to be more authentically Christian than formal Christians, who are still going through the motions of attending their denominations and megachurches, but might as well be attending reformed synagogues. SJWs at least believe in an imminent Heaven on Earth when racism will be banished and Black Lives will Matter. But most formal Christians no longer believe in Heaven – even books on the Rapture do not get $65 million dollar book advances like the PC Saint Obama.

SJWs believe in a Hell, which they see as Western societies that allow on-going 'systemic racism' against the Planet's sacred Earth-People of Color. Formal Christians no longer believe in a Hell of any kind. They have adopted the Jewish view, which is that Hell is merely a place of ghosts, an essentially boring place devoid of pleasure or punishment. SJWs believe in the ancient Christian doctrine of Original Sin, having replaced Adam's disobedience against God with incorrigible whites who disobey Mother Earth. Only whites therefore have Original Sin.

Formal Christians, on the other hand, have entirely abandoned any notion of Original Sin as nothing more than a quaint and psychiatrically unhealthy holdover from the days of myth, many accepting the PC Cult version of sin as 'any expression of Whiteness'. Even the former Ashkenazi specialty of pornography, and the notion of sex as mere recreation, or the Jewish Frankist view that illicit sex brings the End Times closer, have won acceptance among many formal Christians.

In the Middle Ages, Christians would parade a Jew in effigy during holidays as representative of Judas, reinforcing the blood libel that held Jews as a whole responsible for the death of Christ. Christians ceased doing this centuries ago and would not dream of doing such any longer in this age of individualism where collective guilt is seen as profoundly immoral and banned by law. Yet SJWs have happily embraced both collective guilt and blood libel, constantly assaulting whites, burning a white male in effigy at Burning Man (it is never a man-of-color), murdering effigies of every President who refuses to apologize for Whiteness, even attacking him in public plays – especially the 'Nazi' Trump since they saw him as stubbornly encouraging whites to refuse to accept their assigned status of Untouchable.

The PC Cult has thus resurrected the medieval Christian (originally Semitic) tradition of collective guilt and blood libel, holding all whites liable for the crime of Whiteness as the crime of Chaos committed against the Earth Mother and her sacred Earth-People of Color. Again, SJWs show themselves to be more authentically Christian than today's formal Christians. Even their altruism transcends the charity of formal Christians – indeed SJW altruism has no limit.

Therefore, one way or another, former Christians are flocking either to the PC Cult and joining up, ironically preserving much of their Christianity in the process, or they are embracing Israel and nationalistic Israeli Jews, essentially Judaizing in the process. Double irony.

Congressional Democrats hurry to Hollywood, Harvard, and New York to show their obeisance to the Jewish PC priesthood. They know who sets the ideological agenda for the PC Cult, and – just as important – that it is billionaire leftist coastal Jews who write the Democrats' campaign checks.

Congressional Republicans, on the other hand, rush to AIPAC and Israel to show their obeisance to the dual citizen Ziocons; they know that Protestantism and Catholicism have become little more than Jewish heresies, minor Jewish sects with no more to hang their hat on than a shallow doctrine of defenseless, solipsistic Libertarianism that amounts to a Monty Python 'Suicide Squad' from the comedic movie *Life of Brian*.

When the Khazar king converted to Judaism in the 700s, it was not necessary for him to order his subjects to adopt his new faith. The fact of power creates a trickle-down effect that gradually converts all classes to the ruler's new religion, direct coercion being unnecessary. When the Muslims occupied the Middle East and North Africa, they too found it unnecessary to coerce conversion; their taxation of the infidels and the trickle-down effect of their own power persuaded most infidels in time to convert to Islam – even in the face of Muslim policies against conversion as they watched in alarm as their tax revenues collected from Christians and Jews dwindled.

In Washington DC today our ruling elites have become de facto Jews. Republicans openly promote menorahs, embrace Israeli delegations, rush to meet delegations, enthusiastically endorse dual citizenship, suck up to AIPAC, and use American tax money to fund more and more Holocaust Museums in the U.S. though they should be sacred only to Israel, singing the praises of wealthy pro-Israel donors like **Paul Singer** and Sheldon Adelson and Bernie Marcus and Arthur Blank, and of course sending more money to Israel. . . and more money. . . and more money. . .

Trump did this too, and it was politically smart because it is the only effective defense that Republicans have against the Jewish academic priesthood that runs the PC Cult and against Jews who dominate the Beltway, and the only defense Trump had against SJW Jews like George Soros, Michael Bloomberg, Tom

Steyer, Haim Saban, the Sacklers, and the Pritzkers, et al, whose donations maintain the Democratic Party – and maintain the PC Shadow Party that runs the Democratic Party – and subsidize the SJW-infested Deep State.

Outside of DC, SJWs are like Christians in function though not in form. But within the Beltway, SJWs too are becoming de facto Jews, creating for all intents and purposes an American Jewish ruling aristocracy. On the Left, the Democrats and their PC Cult are supported by Far Left wealthy donor Jews. On the Right, the Republicans and their Ziocons are supported by Left of Center wealthy donor Jews. Like the Schiffs, Warburgs, and Rothschilds of history, Michael Bloomberg talks Right but donates Left.

Both Parties therefore are embracing Jews and Judaism since the trickle-down effect of Jewish money and Jewish power in DC makes any alternative electoral strategy unworkable, virtually guaranteeing losing the next election if one so much as hesitates to support another unconstitutional anti-BDS bill, while if one embraces Jewish power then one can remain in office for a lifetime since Democrats consistently block term limits so their SJW leaders will remain irremovable.

With the blessing of the Supreme Court, both parties have embraced the Diversity Cult as America's official State Religion. The elites of both parties know that only by adopting the PC principle of Diversity can they prevent the deck from being stacked against them: the deck of future employment and private lobbying in DC, since, through tribal nepotism, dual citizen Jews now largely staff every Ivy League college, dual citizen Jews head many of the most important Congressional committees, and dual citizen Jewish lawyers and administrators populate every important Deep State bureaucracy, including the intelligence agencies, giving them the ability, if they ever decide to work in concert in DC, to hamstring a President, gridlock Congress, and neutralize the Supreme Court all at the same time – even without the support of SJWs and their PC Cult and their Mass Media. Not that Jew-admiring Republicans would ever lift a finger to stop the penetration of American institutions by Jewish dual citizens, whose primary loyalties are decidedly not to the U.S. They haven't so far.

When the Congress convened in 2020, Democrats and Republicans could not agree on anything, even the time of day – except one: they both agreed that the first act of Congress must be to approve more funding for Israel. Both parties rushed to send delegations to Tel Aviv, competing to offer millions in foreign aid.

One hundred years ago Jews began their rise to the status of an aristocracy in the U.S. They became privileged court advisors under Democrat President Woodrow Wilson in 1917; they ran the White House and the State Department under Democrat President FDR; and they were permanently enthroned in all levels of government by Democrat JFK's rigged election in 1960.

After 1960, it was only a matter of time before the rest of America got the message of who now holds power in DC. As a result of this takeover, the Democratic Party abandoned its long-standing platform of protecting the white working class, and in the mid-1960s switched to the Jewish platform of promoting open borders, sexual perversion, and minority-worship. Seeing the writing on the wall, the Republicans are now doing the same. To do otherwise would mean political suicide by losing the next election in the face of massive funding by the Jewish One Percent of opposing candidates. In this way the white working class was thrown under the bus by both major parties.

Within DC, therefore, the ruling elites, both Democrat and Republican, have subtly embraced Judaism and accepted de facto governance by Jews. Democrats defer to tenured Ivy League Jewish priest-professors of the PC Cult as if they were a source of reliable information, which they are not. Republicans, meanwhile, rush to consult Ziocons and their wealthy Left-of-center Jewish donors and light ever bigger menorahs on the White House lawn while banning Christian crosses from every public building. The Jews who donate to the Democrats match the Jews who donate to their Republican counterparts dollar for dollar. Judaism trickles down the power echelons of DC, following the dictates of money and the collapse of any ideological rival, far quicker and more effectively than in the distant time of the Khazars, but following the same principle of trickle-down power.

Meanwhile, the golem of the PC Cult stumbles on, infecting both parties and every workplace, spreading its illness across the world via school indoctrination and Mass Media, and perhaps deliberately collaborating in unleashing the Coronavirus to cleanse Mother Earth of the aged, removing white Boomers across the world – they may die of the virus, but at least they too won't die as 'racists'. And they can soon be replaced with more compliant immigrants anyway. SJWs always think globally, and when the electorate in a subject province misbehaves, the irremovable SJW leaders replace the electorate.

Infiltrating domestic and international law, the golem stumbles on, there being no independent politicians left in the wasteland of DC to care enough to take notice, much less to do something that might put the golem out of its misery. For instance, by outlawing dual citizenship and all forms of Affirmative Action for 'people of color', including quotas and near-quotas. Outlawing dual citizenship might restore independent national sovereignty to America. Outlawing Affirmative Action, the most destructive social engineering project in the history of America, could finally terminate the Endless Victimization Queue, which is the PC Cult's prime source of recruitment.

Victimhood and having zero children should cease to be economic advantages or. . . well, the future will become a lot poorer, a lot more violent, and a lot darker, literally. But, given that the overturning of *Roe v. Wade* was only a 5-4 decision, and that overturning Affirmative Action – which is currently being decided by the Supreme court as this is being written – will also likely be only a 5-4 majority with many opportunities for being undermined or neutralized by further decisions, one should not conclude that the official state religion of Wokeness can possibly be eliminated by a single SCOTUS decision. Certainly not in the face of widespread electoral fraud. We are in the midst of a religious civil war and it is more likely that the Supreme Court itself will be neutralized than that Affirmative Action, a core value of the PC Cult, will be overturned by any SCOTUS decision.

1 3
JUDAISM AND ISLAM

A few words about Judaism and Islam: The true cultural divide through most of history has been – not Jews and Christians versus Muslims – but Greece and Rome and their progeny versus Judea and Islam and their progeny. This is not primarily a racial division, though that plays a role, but primarily about ideas and history. Not even a thousand years of walling themselves off intellectually from the world in European ghettos were sufficient to make tribal Jews lose their obsession with the Torah and Talmudic Law, just as two centuries of modernization have not sufficed to change Muslims' obsession with their Islamic Law, called the Sharia.

Under both the Talmud and the Sharia, superficial adherence to external form is more important in determining 'correct' adherence to God's commandments than is internal conscience. This is a given. In Islam, one must perform the required duties to Allah called the five pillars, including the *Shahada* (public declaration of faith); *Salat* (the five times daily prayers to Allah; *Sowm* (fasting during Ramadan); *Zakat* (giving alms to the poor); and visiting Mecca for the *Hajj* at least once in one's life, if capable. So long as one performs these duties, while avoiding pork and friendships with non-Muslims, one is a Muslim, and one's place in Paradise is assured, there being no issue with whether one deserves God's grace. Muslims, both Sunni and Shi'i, have elaborated a vast complex of social rules under the Sharia, down to which foot to use when crossing a threshold and which parts of the body to bathe and in which order.

With the Talmud, traditional Jews follow similar highly legalistic restrictions that ensure acceptance by God and His chosen Tribe. Just as Sharia Law is drawn from the Quran, the Sunna, and medieval commentaries, Talmudic Law is drawn from the ancient Torah (first five books of the Old Testament), the medieval Mishna (commentaries of rabbis on the Torah), and the medieval Gemara (legal discussions of the Mishna by rabbis). The process of connecting the Mishnah to the Torah is called *talmud*, from which the entire textual collection eventually came to be called the Talmud. Their analysis is highly legalistic and oriented towards external conformity in a tribal setting, just like the Sharia in Islam, and dictates, for example, that a Jew must not perform any work on the Sabbath, including turning a light switch on or off, which necessitates hiring a 'Shabbas goy', i.e., a Gentile, to do such 'work'.

This prohibition, and similar prohibitions during major Jewish holidays, greatly interferes with farming and historically prevented the development of a Jewish peasantry and has also induced Jews to evade conscription into the militaries of host nations. In Orthodox Judaism, individual conscience takes a distant second place to this superficial compliance with an elaborate set of behavioral rules, discussions of legalistic compliance with the Torah eventually developing into *pilpul*, the Talmudic art of arguing legal disputes merely for the sake of argumentation. Islam's requirement of five times daily prayers has similarly caused economic issues for Muslims, but prayers and the other four duties did not prevent Muslims from farming and developing a prosperous peasantry, and Muslims never developed an art of legal argumentation merely for the sake of argumentation.

Both religions, from public social behavior down to daily prayers are in their essence elaborate rituals designed to impose a duty on God so that God will reward the faithful. In other words, their prayers are magical incantations intended to manipulate God. This is because both religions come from a common Semitic source that emphasizes tribal conformity and manipulative rituals that predate both religions. If an Orthodox Jew or traditional Muslim fails to obtain what he sought after he directed his prayers for that purpose, the fault is ascribed to the believer's failure to perform the supplication in the proper way as required by God. The believer is then obliged to start his prayers over again and 'do it right' so that God will respond favorably. This has similarities with the Jewish medieval Kabbalah.

This conception of the purpose of prayer as manipulative ritual on a contract basis with the Deity is light-years away from the Christian tradition of individual autonomy and controlling the individual through guilt and conscience as opposed to the Semitic tradition of requiring conformity to external tribal rules and legalistic disputes about how best to implement Revealed Holy Law. And as the Christian tradition of envisioning God as the manifestation of a passive Suffering Nature-Deity as opposed to the Semitic tradition of envisioning God as an aggressive, all-powerful Sky-Deity who created and dominates both Nature and Man.

The PC Cult clearly falls directly into the Greek-Christian tradition, its passive Suffering God as a manifestation of Nature easily transforming into a passive Suffering Earth Mother who is One-with-Nature, and who, much like women, suffers as She creates life, having been 'raped' by profane men, and like the Earth itself, is dominated rather than dominates.

The PC Earth Mother is a 'passive-aggressive' divinity, reflected in the daily SJW passive-aggressive behavior of online shadow-banning and constant guilt-tripping and public shaming of heretics. Although Christianity too, especially Catholicism, has had its canon rules of acceptable social behavior and elaborate rituals – just look at the complex schedules of daily celebrations of traditional Catholic nuns – still these do not approach the complexity or have the theological emphasis of Judaism or Islam. In fact, some observers have concluded that Judaism and Islam have no theology because they are free of dogma, asserting that rather than religions *with* law, Judaism and Islam are religions *of* law. This is another way of saying that the formal and the tribal reign supreme in these two Semitic religions.

While the PC Cult definitely has a theology, described in detail earlier, it also has certain parallels with the legalistic orientation of Orthodox Judaism and Islam. This can be seen in the dogma of Intersectionality, and in requiring social behavior proper to one's caste, in its Buddhist-style, drum-circle meditations, and daily recitations of PC prayers like 'Diversity is our strength', 'We are all human', and 'We shall overcome'. A difference between the Cult and Christianity is that, while traditional Christianity has the triune God: God the Father, Jesus the Son, and the Holy Ghost (with Mary Mother of God a subdued 'fourth' divinity), the PC Cult has only One Deity – Mother Mary, who has been Africanized and enthroned as the only God, a Goddess of Nature. Like Islam and Judaism, the PC Cult has just One God, a *female* monotheism. Shrines of the Black Madonna depict Her holding a male infant – this is a holdover from Christianity with the infant 'Christ' having no significance to the Cult except serving to emphasize the character of the Madonna as a mother, making Her a complete woman and Goddess of Creation, much as the Egyptian Isis held the infant Osiris in Her lap.

Just as with Muslims and Orthodox Jews, SJWs have no interest in freedom of speech, voting, juries, or democratic procedures. All of these merely pose risks for the weak in faith to succumb to the temptation of compromise and stray from their irreducible Suffering Black Earth Mother infused with Nietzschean values. This explains why Cult members like Hillary Clinton and John McCain had so little objection to cooperating with traditional Muslims like the Muslim Brotherhood, or with Saudis sympathetic to al-Qaeda, or even working directly with the Islamic State ISIS. They understood each other.

Traditional Muslims also have zero interest in political compromise, democratic procedures, voting, juries, or freedom of speech. These are all *English common law* traditions that are completely alien to the Islamic tradition, and not only to Islam, but also to Orthodox Judaism, and to today's PC Cult, which has its roots in political Socialism and Communism and a defunct Christianity, not in the European Liberal tradition of separation of church and state, or the division of political power exemplified by English democratic traditions stretching back to the Magna

Carta.

This is why the PC Cult's Jihad appears so similar to Islamic Jihad, their members similarly ready to sacrifice themselves for their intolerant Faith. The faiths of the PC Cult and Islam have similar structures. Both are monotheistic, both are formally millenarian, both are absolutist, both demand dedication of one's entire life, there being no aspect of their lives free from its political-religious governance right down to who can use which bathroom. Both faiths have global ambitions, both lack any formal top-down structure like Catholicism, both have no room for political compromise or European-style majoritarian constitutional government, and both demand recognition as the exclusive State Religion, having no tolerance for the notion of separating church from state as enshrined in the American Constitution's First Amendment, and as enshrined in many other Liberal national constitutions.

Indeed, for the PC Cult the very concept of a written Constitution is anathema and SJW leaders repeatedly call for its abolition, and in practice ignore it. A favorite phrase of the early SJW Supreme Court Justice William J. Brennan in regard to the Constitution was, to paraphrase: "It's our Constitution, so we can do with it as we please." And the SJWs on today's Supreme Court do exactly that – as they please, ignoring its actual wording and the intent of the Founders, though the recent reversal of *Roe v. Wade* gives some slight hope that the traditions of English common law embodied in the Constitution may yet survive.

If not for Liberal Rationalism standing between the PC Cult and Islam to serve as a convenient target for both faiths, these two faiths – the matriarchal Earth-centered PC Cult and the patriarchal sky-centered Traditional Islam – would be in a war to the death with each other. Indeed, this is perhaps why Obama declined to terminate the air war against fundamentalist Muslims even while he collaborated with them, despite his friendship with the Muslims Louis Farrakhan and Keith Ellison. Obama, it seems, is more fundamentalist SJW than fundamentalist Muslim.

But inside the borders of the U.S. and the E.U., the PC Cultists and Muslims continue to collaborate to destroy their common enemy: Western democratic Liberalism. Cooperation between these two politicized totalitarian faiths is a repetition of the Red-Brown alliance of the 1930s (Red Communists and Nazi Brownshirts) as today's Leftists, funded by a coterie of Jewish Cultic billionaires, make common cause with traditional Muslims ("our natural allies"), who are funded by both trillionaire Rothschilds and the Saudi royal family. Both work together against European and American democracies.

The so-called 'liberal' Jews under the 'eco-Judaism' label, who helped mastermind the values of the PC Cult, although they may publicly repudiate the Talmud, have not left behind their Orthodox inheritance as much as they suppose – Freud, for example, refused during most of his life to visit the city of Rome due to his hatred of ancient Rome, whose general Titus destroyed the Jewish Temple in 70 AD. And today's 'eco-Jews' are not reproducing themselves like their Orthodox cousins. Around the world, Orthodox and traditional religionists in both Judaism and Islam are having more babies than the 'liberal' or 'reformed' elements in those religions, who embrace gayness and abortion, and limit family size to only one or two children. Eventually Orthodox Jews will greatly outnumber their gay childless PC Jewish cousins.

This trend is pushing ever more traditional religious leaders into power, such as Erdogan in Turkey, who wants to relaunch the traditional Ottoman Caliphate, and is putting ever more restrictive religious policies in force, such as the Haredim in Israel, who along with the Orthodox, have made it a legal requirement for rabbis to approve all Israeli marriages.

This means that the PC Cult, both here in the U.S. and in its local branches in other countries, is also becoming gradually *Judaized* in an Orthodox sense as the larger families, which these conservative elements 'begat', populate inside the PC Cult – or *Islamized* in those areas where Muslim immigrants outnumber Christian-oriented or Jewish-oriented Cult members. Perhaps the tendency of SJW women to favor superficial conformity to make themselves less 'uncomfortable' will eventually translate into a more rules-laden governance of the behavior of SJWs such as prevails in Orthodox Judaism or Islam. In urban centers, it is even becoming common to see 'liberal' white women wearing burkas.

The PC Cult itself, I suspect, though, will in time become more Jewish than Christian in the U.S. as Muslim BDS (Boycott, Divestment, and Sanctions) efforts against Israel are stymied and outlawed by both Democrats and Republicans, and both major parties ever more slavishly submit to Jewish power in DC, continuing their long tradition of 'court Jews'. Today's 'conservative' Christians seem to envisage themselves as imperfect Jews and are clearly reluctant to acknowledge that fear and hatred of Gentiles is an important part of what it means to be a Jew. Therefore, today's Christians seem to have an intrinsic blind spot when it comes to Jewish behavior – they simply cannot see the constant Jewish nurturing of hatred for America and Americans, or recognize that congenital Jewish tribal nepotism has seized the cultural and political heights of American society, which Jews have turned against Americans and their institutions.

Just as today's Diversity-indoctrinated Christians cannot see the sacred rage of Muslims and Muslims' categorical rejection of mixing socially with ritually impure infidels or of participating in infidel institutions, including democratic ones, or the congenital violence that 'desegregation' between Christians and Muslims typically unleashes. In Nigeria this has resulted in the deaths of tens of thousands in huge riots over the decades, just as racial de-segregation in the American South unleashed a permanent, slow-motion murderous *pogrom* by blacks against whites with U.S. government aid, which has resulted in the violent deaths of thousands of whites at the hands of blacks, amounting to far more deaths than the sum total of lynchings of blacks by whites in former times.

It is a safe bet, therefore, that whichever influence comes to dominate within the PC Cult – totalitarian Christianity fallen into a Black Hole, or totalitarian Judaism increasingly Messianic and Orthodox – the PC Cult will remain devoted to White Genocide as its SJW believers, under the influence of Jewish-owned and Jewish-controlled education and media, embrace their own destruction with ever more enthusiasm, and as American blacks ethnically cleanse more and more cities of whites rendered legally defenseless by the Cultic Justices on the Supreme Court, while both Jews and Muslims look on these developments with happy approval.

Perhaps what is needed is neither Judaism nor Christianity but a return to the principles that originally made Greece and Rome great. When faced with existential challenges from the Semitic world, Rome did not imagine that coexistence was possible. It did not sink into sterile pacifism and turn the other cheek in the face of Semitic aggression. Rome *annihilated* Carthage and sowed salt in its ruins, and later destroyed Jerusalem and permanently banned Jews from the city and constructed its own pagan temple to Jupiter where the Jewish Temple had once been. As a result, Europe survived free of Asian domination for centuries, defying invasions by Persians, Muslims, Mongols, and Turks, and imposing permanent legal disabilities on disloyal resident Jews.

Today the new threats to the West are no longer Mongols or Turks, but Tel Aviv and Mecca. Both, along with today's corrupted Christianity, the bastard offshoot of Judaism and the Jews' first slave-morality-infused Golem (the first of many), are more of an existential challenge to Europe and the Western world than were Carthage or ancient Jerusalem.

Will the modern West produce leaders who have the courage and strength to do what the Romans did when faced with similar existential threats? Far from terminating the influence of Tel Aviv and Mecca and reversing the Semitic influences – manifest today as the creeping totalitarian Asian despotism of the PC Cult infiltrating the West via a corrupt and moribund pseudo-Christianity under Jewish leadership – today's leaders can no longer preserve their borders from invasion by millions of equatorial migrants who openly proclaim their hatred of the West and Westerners even while they invade and occupy it.

What for centuries had been seen as positive traits in the West's Faustian civilization: tolerant colonial mandates over backward peoples; imperial control of peaceful global trade routes; internal ethnic cohesion; loyalty and honor in natural hierarchical organizations; racial pride and consciousness; masculinity as the engine of creation responsible for inventing the combustion engine, computers, cars, cell phones, science, medicine, and the entire apparatus of modern civilization (now culturally appropriated by SJWs and used to attack the very same discoverers and inventors); exploration and expansion into every locale, even to the Moon and Mars; acknowledging and admiring capable bloodlines; limiting the reproduction of bad bloodlines; segregation of sexes and races to preserve the confidence and ability of youth; preservation of national resources and national borders; outlawing abortion and sexual perversion as threats to the essential reproductive core of society; enforcing a quick death penalty to avoid life-criminals gaining control over prisons and courts via threats to the families of employees and judges, as has happened in Mexico and elsewhere – all these have suddenly been absurdly labeled by the Diversity Cult as Evil 'Whiteness', and centuries of hard-won experience and hyper-success have been recklessly discarded as 'systemic' voodoo. And they wonder why suicide and crime and corruption and self-mutilation have become suddenly epidemic.

Where is the Leader who can restore sovereignty to the West, renew its Faustian fertility, and by any means remove SJWs and their PC Death Cult, along with its fellow-traveler treasonous dual citizens, who together are responsible for the West's decline? Where are our Scipios who destroyed Semitic Carthage to its roots, our Titus who demolished the Semitic Jewish Temple, our Jan Sobieski who saved Vienna from the Muslim Turks, our Templars who defeated them at Malta, our Richard the Lionheart who defeated Saladin? Where is our El Cid who gave his life to fight the Muslims in Spain, our Charles Martel who halted the Muslims at Tours preventing Muslim occupation of all Europe? Where is our Ivan the Great who conquered and demolished the Mongol cities of Kazan and Astrakhan halting centuries of Mongol and Muslim slave-predation of whites in Russia, a predation that originated the word 'slave', which for a thousand years was a synonym for White Europeans abducted by Asians and Africans, until Europeans finally halted the traffic by military force? Where is our Franco who saved Spain from the golem of Marxian Socialism, our Pinochet who did the same for Chile, our Mussolini who attempted to spread Roman civilization in the Mediterranean and who was hung upside down for his efforts? Where is our Leon Degrelle who was wounded six times fighting the Bolsheviks in Russia? Where is our Hitler who inflicted a mortal blow against the totalitarian Bolshevism that had seized control of Russia, thus preserving most of Europe from enslavement by Asian despotism for more than a generation? Where are leaders like these who were willing to fight to preserve and renew Western Civilization? And where is our 'pagan' European religion that can reverse the tide of despotic Asian Abrahamic cults with a tolerant polytheism whose roots lie in the Indo-European culture that once united all Europe?

14
AFTERTHOUGHTS

Most of this book was written at the height of the Wuhan Coronavirus, which it now appears may well have been a product of
American bioweapons research. (See the recent work of Ron Unz
at www.unz.com). The stock market has crashed – as I predicted
it would since the massive transfer of wealth from the public to
the One Percent effected by the Cult-dominated Federal Reserve
could not last forever. The bubble of artificially inflated asset
prices as connected insiders used the Fed's tsunami of free money
to buy back corporate shares and pocket the huge bonuses that
rising stock prices created for them, instead of using the Fed's
free money to improve their businesses and prepare for the inevitable downturn, it seems has finally been pricked.

Due to the Fed's largesse, many CEOs, like Michael
Bloomberg, have effortlessly become multi-billionaires while the
American middle class were forced from their homes into growing tent cities by skyrocketing housing prices, declining wages,
and exploding taxes. This looting by the One Percent was enabled
by the PC Cult's python-like stranglehold over the U.S. government, the Democratic Party's worship of perpetual and exponen-
tial deficit spending, and the Republican Party's love affair with
cheap immigrant labor and the export of jobs.

The looting of America by the Fed – a private trust of interlocked banks – in partnership with Wall Street and both political

parties will only increase as the government embraces deficit spending without limit, known as MMT, in desperate efforts to prop up stock prices to keep the looting going as long as possible. With multiple top Blackrock executives embedded in Biden's administration, and yet another national election swindled in 2022, it is certain that the looting will continue. As long as the Religion of Diversity remains the state religion of the West, and as long as Cult members control all levers of power, the destruction of the White Middle Class in America will continue and will follow the already-sacrificed White Working Class, abandoned by both parties fifty years ago, into oblivion.

The Virus was perhaps inevitable because it is nature's way of reducing excess population and more viruses will follow. Whether the U.S. was responsible for creating the bioweaponed virus, its damage on the U.S. and on Western societies was made possible only by the Cult's policy of open borders, globalism, and unrestrained immigration – SJW federal judges illegally canceled Trump's 'racist' efforts to restrict flights from China *even in the midst of the virus outbreak.* And the timing of the virus is suspicious insofar as the first person to fly into the U.S. from Wuhan on January 15, 2020, departed for the U.S. the same day that SJW Speaker of the House Pelosi, after delaying for weeks, finally sent her Impeachment Articles to the Senate, knowing that the Senate would vote it down. In other words, the virus was given a free ride to enter the U.S. as soon as it became clear that Pelosi's Impeachment had failed.

The globalist PC Cult has long maintained working alliances with every enemy of the U.S., including the Chinese Communist

Party, which perhaps deliberately transmitted the virus to the U.S. in an American election year after all efforts to remove the 'heretic' Trump had failed, a virus that mostly affects the aging Boomer (i.e., White Middle Class) generation. China might welcome the removal of its older generation; but the West stands to lose its most experienced and knowledgeable cadres.

Whether designed as a bioweapon or not – and, like with the French Revolution, it is way too soon to tell – after ignoring the crime, disease, domestic shootings, collapsed institutions, trashed environment, corruption, loss of respect for law and order, drug abuse, and suicides brought by its Globalism so far, the Cult is being forced to face the consequences of its globalist agenda. The Virus, however, will doubtless not prove fatal to the Cult because the Cult is about values and beliefs, not expediencies. There are no such things as human beings without myth, and no such thing as a true atheist – *humans without religious myth are the ultimate contradiction in terms*.

This is Nietzsche's most important insight, which SJWs at large, and Americans in particular, obsessed as they are with science and engineering instead of ideas and contemplating the harsh lessons of history, cannot seem to grasp. No one is immune to religious fanaticism and the Cult is now the dominant Religious Myth in the West. Therefore, as the Virus retreats and normal life resumes, as is now finally happening, the Cult's open borders and unrestrained immigration will also resume – probably with even greater emphasis on massive southerly immigration with the excuse that more immigration than ever will be necessary for business revival.

This too will be a lie. The Cult depends on lies. More immigration means more viruses, lower wages, and more social disturbance. Even the Cult media's naming of the virus as 'the Coronavirus' – when there are many known coronaviruses but only one first identified in Wuhan, and when most epidemics are routinely named after the place of origin, like Ebola and Zika – reflects the Cult's stranglehold over the mind of the West. Until the religion of pretend Equality and fake Diversity is extinguished from the life of America and the West, enabling the West to finally regenerate, the genocide of whites – the true goal of SJWs and their PC Cult – will continue, and already seems to have risen to a new level with the Cult-inspired conflict in Ukraine, where President **Zelensky**, his billionaire patron **Ihor Kolomoisky**, and SJW U.S. Ambassador **Victoria Nuland**, all Jews, provoked a Russian invasion that is killing no one but whites.

Indeed, one may be certain that even as the Ukraine war is blamed on Russia, the Cult will find a way to blame the Wuhan Virus on the U.S., because, in renewed efforts to complete its genocide, in the mythic mind of SJWs, Whiteness equals Chaos and the Africanized Great Earth Mother – their Black Madonna – cannot coexist with Chaos but must destroy Chaos in order to create its New World Order, the SJWs' Heaven on Earth. This can only come about if all whites, including both Ukraine and Russia, are subjected to genocide by massive southerly immigration, abortion, and the full panoply of destructive PC Cult policies.

BIBLIOGRAPHY

Adorno, Theodor W., *The Authoritarian Personality* (The American Jewish Committee, 1950)

Aronowitz, Stanley, *The Crisis in Historical Materialism: Class, Politics and Culture in Marxist Theory* (Praeger, 1981)

Bernays, Edward, *Propaganda* (1928) (Edward Bernays, 2019, reprint from 1928)

Bloom, Allan, *The Closing of the American Mind* (Simon & Schuster, 1987)

Bork, Robert H., *The Tempting of America: The Political Seduction of the Law* (Simon & Schuster, 1990)

Buchanan, Patrick J., *Suicide of a Superpower* (St. Martin's Press, 2011)

Buchanan, Patrick J., *Churchill, Hitler and "The Unnecessary War"* (Three Rivers Press, 2008)

Campbell, Joseph, *The Masks of God: Creative Mythology* (Penguin Books, 1968)

Chapin, Bernard, *SJWs Attack* (2019).

Chesler, Phyllis, *Mothers On Trial: The Battle for Children and Custody* (The Seal Press, 1986)

Cochran, Gregory & Henry Harpending, *The 10,000 Year Ex-*

plosion: How Civilization Accelerated Human Evolution (Basic Books, 2009)

www.Counter-Currents.com

Crump, David, Eugene Gressman, David S. Day, *Cases and Materials on Constitutional Law, 3rd Ed.* (Matthew Bender, 1998)

Day, Vox, *SJWs Always Lie* (Catalia House, 2013)

Day, Vox, *SJWs Always Double Down: Anticipating the Thought Police* (Catalia House, 2015)

Draper, Theodore, *American Communism and Soviet Russia: The Formative Period* (Octagon Books, 1977, reprint from 1960) (See especially the chapter "The Negro Question")

Durkheim, Émile, *The Rules of Sociological Method, 8th Ed.* (The Free Press, 1938)

Dutton, Edward, *Making Sense of Race* (Washington Summit, 2020)

Eliade, Mircea, *The Myth of the Eternal Return, or Cosmos and History* (Princeton Univ. Press, 1954)

Eliade, Mircea, Patterns in Comparative Religion (Univ. of Nebraska Press, 1958)

Ennes, James M., *Assault on the Liberty: The True Story of the Israeli Attack on an American Intelligence Ship* (Random House, 1979)

Evola, Julius, *Revolt Against The Modern World* (Inner Traditions International, 1969)

www.FightWhiteGenocide.com

Fitgerald, F. Scott, *The Great Gatsby* (Simon & Schuster, 1991, original copyright 1925)

Fitzpatrick, Sheila, Ed., *Cultural Revolution in Russia: 1928-1931* (Indiana Univ. Press, 1978)

Flaherty, Colin, *Don't Make the Black Kids Angry: The Hoax of Racial Victimization and How We Enable It* (Mighty-Right Media, 2015)

Flaherty, Colin, *White Girl Bleed a Lot* (WND Books, 2013)

Gilman, Sander L., *Jewish Self-Hatred* (Johns Hopkins Univ. Press, 1986)

Goad, Jim, Whiteness: *The Original Sin* (Obnoxious Books, 2018)

Goldberg, Jonah, *Liberal Fascism: The Secret History of the American Left, from Mussolini to the Politics of Change* (Broadway Books, 2007)

Griffin, G. Edward, *The Creature From Jekyll Island: A Second Look at the Federal Reserve* (American Media, 2010)

Heller, Michail & Aleksandr M. Nekrich, *Utopia in Power: The History of the Soviet Union From 1917 to the Present* (Summit Books, 1982)

www.heretical.com

Herrnstein, Richard J. & Charles Murray, *The Bell Curve* (The Free Press, 1994)

Horowitz, David & Richard Poe, *The Shadow Party: How George Soros, Hillary Clinton, and Sixties Radicals Seized Control of the Democratic Party* (Thomas Nelson, 2006)

Huntington, Samuel P., *The Clash of Civilizations and the Remaking of World Order* (Simon & Schuster, 1996)

Jarvie, I.C., *The Revolution in Anthropology* (Regnery, 1964)

Jayman's Human Biodiversity Blog (www. jaymans.wordpress. com)

Johnson, Greg, *The White Nationalist Manifesto* (Counter-Currents Publishing, 2018)

Johnson, Paul, *Intellectuals* (Harper & Row, 1988)

Kolakowski, Leszek, *Main Currents of Marxism: Its Origins, Growth and Dissolution* (Oxford Univ. Press, 1978) 3 volumes.

Labedz, Leopold, Ed., *Revisionism: Essays on the History of Marxist Ideas* (Frederick A. Praeger, 1962)

LaHaye, Tim, *The Battle for the Family* (Power Books, 1982)

Laqueur, Walter, *A History of Zionism* (Schocken Books, 1972)

MacDonald, Kevin, *The Culture of Critique* (1st Books, 1998, rev'd 2002)

MacKinnon, Catherine A., *Toward a Feminist Theory of the State* (Harvard Univ. Press, 1989)

Marcus, George E., Michael M.J. Fischer, *Anthropology as Cultural Critique* (Univ. of Chicago Press, 1986)

Marcuse, Herbert, *Eros and Civilization: A Philosophical Inquiry Into Freud* (Beacon Press, 1955)

Martin, Tony, *The Jewish Onslaught, 3rd Ed.* (Majority Press, 1994)

Nietzsche, Friedrich, *The Birth of Tragedy* (Penguin Books, 1991)

Nietzsche, Friedrich, *Daybreak* (Cambridge, 1997)

Nietzsche, Friedrich, *The Gay Science* (Cambridge, 2001)

Nietzsche, Friedrich, *Human, All-Too-Human & Beyond Good And Evil* (Wordsworth Classics, 2008)

Nietzsche, Friedrich, *Thus Spake Zarathustra* (Cambridge, 2006)

Nietzsche, Friedrich, *Twilight of the Idols & The Anti-Christ* (Penguin Books, 1968)

Nietzsche, Friedrich, *The Will To Power* (Penguin Books, 2017)

O'Brien, David M., *Storm Center: The Supreme Court in American Politics, 3rd Ed.* (W.W. Norton & Co., 1993)

O'Neill, William L., *A Better World: The Great Schism – Stalinism and the American Intellectuals* (Simon & Schuster, 1982)

www.OccidentalDissent.com

www.TheOccidentalObserver.net

Otto, Rudolf, *The Idea of the Holy* (Oxford Univ. Press, 2nd ed., 1950)

Presser, Stephen B. & Jamil S. Zainaldin, *Law and Jurisprudence in American History: Cases & Materials, 4th Ed.* (West Group, 2000)

Pinker, Steven, *The Blank Slate: The Modern Denial of Human Nature* (Penguin Books, 2002)

Raspail, Jean, *The Camp of the Saints* (The Social Contract Press, 2018, reprint from 1973)

Sachar, Abram Leon, *A History of the Jews, 5th Ed.* (Alfred A. Knopf, 1967)

Schorske, Carl E., *Fin-De-Siecle Vienna: Politics and Culture* (Vintage Books, 1981)

Sepehr, Robert, *1666 Redemption Through Sin* (Atlantean Gardens, 2015)

www.ShrinesoftheBlackMadonna.org (recently switched to www.linktr.ee/sobm)

Solomon, Robert C., *From Rationalism to Existentialism: The Existentialists and Their Nineteenth-Century Backgrounds* (Humanities Press, 1970)

Solzhenitsyn, Alexander, *Двести Лет Вместе* (Vremya, 2015) 2 Volumes. Trans: *Two Hundred Years Together*.

Spengler, Oswald, *The Decline of the West* (Alfred A. Knopf, 1926, 1928) 2 Volumes

Spengler, Oswald, *The Hour of Decision* (Isha Books, 2013, reprint from 1934)

Stent, Gunther S., *Paradoxes of Progress* (W.H. Freeman & Co.,

1978)

Steyn, Mark, *America Alone* (Regnery, 2006)

Strauss, Leo, *Natural Right and History* (Univ. of Chicago Press, 1953)

Trotsky, Leon, *The Permanent Revolution & Results and Prospects* (Merit Publishers, 1969)

Ulam, Adam B., *The Bolsheviks* (Collier Books, 1965)

Ulam, Adam B., *Expansion and Coexistence: Soviet Foreign Policy, 1917-73*, 2nd Ed. (Praeger, 1974)

United Nations, Human Development Report 2019

www.unz.com

Wade, Nicholas, *A Troublesome Inheritance: Genes, Race and Human History* (Penguin Books, 2015)

Watson, James D., Gunther S. Stent, Ed., *The Double Helix: A Personal Account of the Discovery of the Structure of DNA* (W.W. Norton, 1980)

Weiss, Bernard G., *The Spirit of Islamic Law* (Univ. of Georgia Press, 1998)

Wilson, E.O., *Consilience: The Unity of Knowledge* (Vintage Books, 1999)

Wilson, E.O., *Sociobiology: The New Synthesis* (Harvard Univ. Press, 1975)

Wolfe, Bertram D., *An Ideology in Power: Reflections on the*

Russian Revolution (Stein & Day, 1969)

Yockey, Francis P., *Imperium* (Invictus Books, 2011; original publication 1948)

If you enjoyed this book, please visit

www.sirius.reviews

www.ingramcontent.com/pod-product-compliance
Lightning Source LLC
Chambersburg PA
CBHW060846280326
41934CB00007B/933